Mama Gena's School of Womanly Arts

Using the Power of Pleasure to Have Your Way with the World

Regena Thomashauer

SIMON & SCHUSTER
NEW YORK LONDON TORONTO SYDNEY SINGAPORE

SIMON & SCHUSTER
Rockefeller Center
1230 Avenue of the Americas
New York, NY 10020

Designed by Jan Pisciotta

For information about special discounts for bulk purchases,
please contact Simon & Schuster Special Sales:
1-800-456-6798 or business@simonandschuster.com.

Manufactured in the United States of America

1 3 5 7 9 10 8 6 4 2

Library of Congress Cataloging-in-Publication Data
Thomashauer, Regena.
Mama Gena's School of Womanly Arts : using the power of pleasure
to have your way with the world / Regena Thomashauer.
p. cm.
1. Women—Psychology. 2. Women—Conduct of life. 3. Pleasure.
4. Self-realization. I. Title.
HQ1206 .T4673 2002
305.4—dc21
2002017687

ISBN 0-7432-2684-4

Acknowledgments

I thank my daughter, Maggie, for the gift of Motherhood. I thank her for making me aware of the link between me and the ancestresses who have gone before me and made me possible, and to the girls of now, and the women to come. I thank her for her love, and the joy of loving her.

To my Dad who always said I should be a writer. Thank you. You were right.

To my Mom, for her beauty, her sparkle, her flirtatiousness, her vision, and her deep, deep love.

To Steve and Vera Bodansky who awakened slumbering aspects of my soul with their love. Thank you for opening the doors to my passion. You inspire me every day.

To J.B. and Laura, the most magnificent, steadfast friends who taught me so much about the love and fun that a man and woman can create in relationship.

To Anh Duong who drives me higher, challenges me, and has opened my vistas to beauty and extraordinary friendship.

To Peter McGough, my soul's playmate. Thank you, dear friend.

To my protégée, Auntie Beth Schoenfeldt, who makes sure I operate at full-throttle Sister Goddess power. Thank you for your willingness to leap in the direction of your desires, despite being from Texas.

Thank you to my T.I.G.R.E.S.S.es—Meryl Ranzer, Jennifer Freeman, Laleh Nader, Lori Sutherland, Sharon Friedland, Alice Petzold, Laura Tulumbus, and especially Rhea Abramson for being my research assistant.

To Jen Gates, my agent. (Oh, what a thrill it is to have an agent. . . .)

For "getting me"—right away, at the beginning—and making sure everyone else did, too.

To Amanda Murray, my hot, sexy editor. Thank you for a dream-come-true collaboration, and for my love affair with your mind. I appreciate your willingness to enter my world in order to make this book great.

To Patrick and Walter Fleming, to Brian Bradley and Josh Patner for the clothes—the magnificent, magical clothes.

And to all my Sister Goddesses, now, and forever.

This book is dedicated to my husband, Bruce, whose love for me makes all this, and me, not only possible but an astonishingly glorious adventure, for which I am profoundly grateful. He loves every fiber of my being, and presses me to reach for more than I could have dreamed. He rejoices in and encourages my passion, my outrageousness, my irrepressible adventurousness. He asks for nothing in return, but the privilege of loving me. I am now, and forever, at his feet.

Author's Note

The stories about people told in this book reflect feelings or situations which many of us have experienced in our own lives. While the essence of the stories is real, many are composites and, in most cases, names of individuals and other characteristics have been changed.

Contents

Mama Gena's School of Womanly Arts

Introduction

Have no fear, Mama Gena is here! This book is your road map to the heart and soul, the scintillating core, of being a woman. It's the result of twelve years' research into what women want and what makes us happy. It's a how-to guide for living a completely fulfilled life.

Sounds good, doesn't it?

The key to this wonderful life is what I call the "womanly arts"—a set of skills and behaviors that you already know but may have forgotten about. If practiced passionately and enthusiastically, these arts allow every woman to revel in her own fabulousness. They give her the power to create a life of pleasure, abundance, and full gratification.

* * *

I want you to start thinking about the life you would have if you could. I want you to envision your own fantasyland. Give free rein to this vision of your desired lifestyle, and don't let it be dominated by someone else's plans for you. Do you see a life that allows for for intimacy, family, responsibility, creativity, great sex, flexible time, and flexible emotions? Do you see days filled with alone time—or shared activities with a bevy of friends, family, and children? Do you see hours spent volunteering, or making big bucks in a high-powered career, or creating the next great painting or novel? Do you see yourself in a rural place, or by the beach, or up in the mountains, or in a small town, or in a city apartment? Do you see a life spent with one love, or filled with a myriad of interesting and exciting partners?

Maybe you see yourself picking a bit of this and dash of that.

Whatever your vision is, however unlikely, unorthodox, or "unacceptable," get ready to run with it. Your feelings are the utmost priority, your desires are more important than anyone else's deadline or mandate.

A pleasurable life is not a necessity. Not an obligation. We are taught to work hard, study hard, and deprive ourselves. But who teaches us about pleasure? Who teaches us to laugh when we feel like it, to concentrate on how good the sun feels on our skin, to value the giddy pleasure of playing hooky, or to plunge forward enthusiastically and seize our own brass ring? Many of us have almost forgotten a life of pleasure can exist. As a woman, though, pleasure is your birthright. That's the big, fat secret I am here to unlock with you.

Your dreams, your desires are not too big for you. They are just the right size. And they are rapidly and readily accessible if you follow me through the doorway of pleasure. This doorway has always been there—Mama is just reminding you where the key is and giving you a little shove toward happiness and success, however you define them. I am here to tell you that every woman can be creative, sexy, and happy and can have a marvelous relationship with a life partner. Glamour and beauty are within reach. And ecstasy, pleasure, and fun can play a huge role in your life.

In working with countless women as a facilitator and researcher in the area of relationships, I have discovered that a woman's pleasure has an electrifying effect on herself and others. If a woman even begins to think about what pleasures her, she instantly feels pleasured. And if that woman can communicate those delicious thoughts to someone else, that lucky person also feels the glow. I know, I know, it sounds so simple. But hey, no one is in the habit of looking at the power of pleasure.

So many people have dedicated themselves to examining women's problems and making much of their general unhappiness. Therapists, weight-loss centers, credit card companies—everybody's got us in their clutches, and somehow women as a whole aren't too much happier for it. I dedicated so much time to studying women's unhappiness (my own included), and none of it led to fun. Finally I decided to investigate women's pleasure instead. No one else was doing it, really. It was a wide-open field, no competition. Not too many people seemed to have the time or the interest to explore pleasure—how to attain it and the rewards that come with it. And what I have found has proved to be amazing, beyond anything I could have dreamed. I learned that the pleasure women are capable of—that energy—is the greatest untapped natural resource on this planet. I discovered that when a woman is happy and fulfilled, those around her share the rewards. A gratified woman can be the source of a whole community's joy and prosperity.

That revelation led me to study what I call the womanly arts—the skills that enable us to access joy, gratification, energy, and fun all day, every day. Here's a rundown:

- The first and most important womanly art is the ability to identify your desires. Mama is here to help you locate what you really want and show you how to *whet your own appetite.* Some women (maybe most women) don't even know what they want. We will coddle your fledgling desires until they sing to you loud and clear.

- The second womanly art is the art of *having fun,* no matter where you are. I'll help you figure out a way to have a good time whether you're at the dry cleaner, sitting at your desk, listening to your mother-in-law, or doing your taxes.

- The third womanly art I'll talk about is the art of *sensual pleasure.* The orientation to pleasure is a feminine instinct, and each glorious inch of your body is yours to use for your fulfillment. Women have a greater affinity for pleasure—a drive, an innate understanding of pleasure—simply because they're women. After all, they have an organ on their body whose sole function is pleasure. You will learn more about your instrument and its potential.

- *Flirting* is another womanly art. It is a fantastic way to fire up your entire life. When a woman has mastered her ability to flirt, she feels deliciously powerful.

- When you feel good enough to flirt, you feel good enough to practice the womanly art of *owning your beauty.* Mama will inspire you to make the decision, every minute of every day, that you are the hottest, most gorgeous thing that ever lived. Why not? You are.

- I will also encourage you to *befriend your inner bitch.* Learning to live with her is an art. And as you know, if you're heading into battle you want that bitch on your side! Mama will show you how.

- *Owning and operating men* is another womanly art. You already knew that. We'll investigate the ways in which a woman's pleasure (namely, yours) can help both of you live happily ever after.

- And the final womanly art we'll be learning is the art of *inviting abundance.* Women have uncanny powers of attraction. You'll learn how to conjure up anything you want—a new coat, a parking space, a new job for your best friend.

In this book Mama will articulate all the skills, the opportunities, and the pathways a woman can access to become enthusiastically gratified. Along the way we will explore your deepest intuitions, your desires both great and small, and pleasure—as experienced by all your five senses. I'll show you the power that comes when you embrace all of your contradictions—when you let Elegant and Slutty sit side by side, or allow Tacky, Tasteful, Over-the-top, and Understated to appear simultaneously, in the same ball gown. We'll put Shy in her proper place, next to Abandon. We'll invite unabashed Hilarity to disrupt the most refined dinner tables. You'll see Voracious and Virginal are not incompatible. In these pages, Lust is exalted, Repression abhorred. The fragrance of freshly sweaty skin is more divinely valuable than Chanel No. 5.

You'll soon learn that anything fun is preferable to a dozen obligations, and in my book, a shot of fulfillment is always the next best step. I'll help you realize that there is always time for passion, in any form. And gratitude. Showers of gratitude and thanks are the order of the day.

To embrace the womanly arts, you must simply begin with a positive point of view. Rely on the fact that something good or something better than good is heading your way at all times. Your manicured hand is in control of your own ecstasy dial. Whatever befalls you, you can and will use it to make yourself happy. In every circumstance you are the one with the edge. You will know that whatever your desires are, they will not just be fulfilled, but bettered and expanded, with frosting on top. Most women spend their time whining about the past rather than paying attention to what they want now. What you will soon see is that ecstasy comes from leaping in the direction of your desires, despite the obstacles. What might surprise you most is that true selfishness can be the path to real generosity.

We are going to bypass doubt, judgment, and disapproval. We are going to leave the past where it is and enjoy the present even more by focusing on rituals, exercises, and new perspectives that introduce your dreams and your desires right into reality, *right now.* You are about to be a gratified woman. A gratified woman can have a glorious time washing the dishes, changing a tire, or being ravished in bed. Being on intimate terms with joy, she can create it anywhere. She is not limited by circumstances, money, education, background, or geography. She does not have to find the "right" guy to have a great evening out—she can draw out the best in any man. She does not need the latest fashion to feel beautiful—she knows her glow comes from within, no matter what she is wearing.

A gratified woman is someone who constantly experiences the abundance of life itself and the privilege of life itself because she knows that wherever she is, just by the force of nature that is her being, anything is possible. And that is a wonderful place to be. If you are ready to live in this place, if you are ready for unbridled joy and overflowing passion regardless of life's challenges, turn the page and start the course—the course of succulence, the course of outrageousness, the course I call Mama Gena's School of Womanly Arts.

Lesson 1

The Case for Pleasure

I felt it was time to play. Most of my thoughts, time and energy had gone into creative effort. And this restriction of the love drive, the headshrinkers will tell you, is the greatest urge one really has. When one sublimates the sex drive into creative work it puts a person in high gear, mentally. I admit it. But it is against my nature to bottle up the biological plans of pleasure for any length of time. I hope I don't sound as if I have discovered the secret salve that soothes the universe, but I do want to add my small footnote on the subject.

—Mae West

Example A. Picture this:

You are on a long road trip, in a car, by yourself. You're kind of hungry, kind of cranky, but too impatient to get where you're going to stop at a rest area. You keep pushing yourself, ignoring your discomfort, so you can cover more distance.

Example B. Picture this:

You are on a long road trip, in a car, with a couple of girlfriends. Each of you packed a basket of delicious goodies to snack on, and you are currently passing around some crudités with guacamole. Aretha is blasting on the radio, and some of you are singing along. You have a stack of CDs, books on tape, and *The Story of O.* You have a destination, but you keep stopping at all the interesting sites along the way—shopping malls, and places called Lost River Caverns and The World's Only Anchovy Museum.

Which trip would you rather be on, A or B?

B? Good choice. Know why?

B gets there first. Know why?

Since A began to ignore how she was feeling about a hundred miles ago, she failed to notice the engine light on the dashboard, so the car overheated, and now she's sitting by the side of the road, cursing and waiting for Triple A to come rescue her.

This illustrates two options: *a life without pleasure* and *a life that includes pleasure.*

In this lesson we are going to tour the world of pleasure together. We will examine everything that qualifies as part of a pleasurable life. Why? Pleasure gives you clarity, it refreshes and rejuvenates, it keeps you ahead of the curve. Pleasure sends you on wonderful journeys, and you always arrive at your destination ahead of schedule. When you don't prioritize pleasure, you end up arriving in places you never intended to go. So many of us are programmed to choose A in the scenario above that we suffer from the disease called *anhedonia* (literally, "without pleasure"). A leading American manual on mental illness describes it as "a loss of interest or pleasure in all or almost all usual activities and pastimes." People give up on fun. Making time for pleasure seems somehow naughty, self-indulgent, or slightly illicit.

Society conditions us to worship pain. "No pain, no gain." It's everywhere: Jesus nailed to the cross, original sin, the Puritan work ethic. Who goes out for a lunch hour anymore? (We used to.) Who comes home from work at 5 P.M.? (That's only half a day!) Even our pals in Latin America are giving up that centuries-old ritual, the siesta. And we used to laugh at how hard the Japanese work. Now we have surpassed them.

Pleasure is still there. It is simply not a priority. Reveling in it is a lost art. All you have to do is look at a child and you will see the direct access we all have to pleasure. A child moves from one pleasurable thing to another, gets interrupted with a few tears, a distraction, then back to pleasure. Pleasure is more important than food. Pleasure consumes a child's day. Pleasure is not frivolous. It guides, instructs, unfolds creativity, educates. Learning through pleasure, through fun, is a more deeply integrated experience than learning by rote or under pressure.

The idea for Mama Gena's School of Womanly Arts came to me after seeing Jacqueline Bisset in the movie *Dangerous Beauty* utter these words to her daughter, who she was training to be a courtesan: "In order to give pleasure, you have to know pleasure." It was a very beautiful scene, set in sixteenth-century Venice. I was captivated by the idea of a gorgeous, sensual mother sharing the secrets of pleasure and sensuality with her daughter. Why, if that had happened to me, I could have hit the ground running after puberty, rather than spend years mired in confusion and misinformation. Imagine having your mom teach you how to enjoy the touch, taste, and smell of kissing your first boy! Or how peeling an orange or eating an asparagus spear can be a method of seduction. Or how your eyes, the windows of your soul, can be used to ignite a flirtation. Imagine having your mama in your corner as you begin your sensual unfolding. How delicious, and how totally unusual.

I had found my calling. The Pleasure Queen. The epiphany was brought on by a convergence of sorts. I had recently become a mama. My husband, Bruce, and I had been teaching courses together in sensuality, communication, and relationships for about seven years, and I had been feeling lately that there was something I wanted to say to women, in the presence of women only. I had also been studying the ancient Goddess religions as a kind of hobby. I realized the golden thread winding through all of my experience and research at that point was the divine importance of pleasure. Female pleasure. The next thing you know, Mama Gena and her School of Womanly Arts was born.

There was a time, five thousand years ago, and for about thirty to fifty centuries before that, when humanity worshiped a female deity. God was a Goddess. From the scant little we know about those fantastically good old days, it seems religious practices were quite a bit different than they are these days. There was dancing, celebration of the seasons, and sensuality, abundant thanks and adoration, ecstatic emotion. Really not at all like what shakes in our shrines nowadays. Now it's all about men—here a rabbi, there a pope, everywhere a monk monk. In the old days there was no sitting still and being quiet and repenting, no guilt about original or unoriginal sins. I was inspired by the idea of a gratitude festival in honor of the gift of life. And that's how the Goddess came to be such a powerful theme in Mama Gena's School of Womanly Arts. I call the participants in the course my Sister Goddesses to remind us that all women on this planet are sisters and all are descendants of Goddess worshipers. In fact, we are Goddesses all. Now that's just Mama's opinion. But think about it: treat a woman like a Goddess, she rises to the occasion. That's a tip that will take men far in the world of women. Worship her, and she will give you the best she's got.

As a Sister Goddess, I have made pleasure the guiding principle in my life and the lives of my family, and in my business. If something does not feel good, we don't do it. If it feels good, we do. And because no action would feel good if it hurt or compromised someone else, pleasure is moral in the highest sense of the word.

All you have to do is choose to feel good. Pleasure is a choice, just as hatred or unhappiness is a choice. Pleasure is not necessarily in the results, like getting a promotion or the right job; pleasure is not just an aftereffect of getting a raise, so that you are making the same amount of money as the guy in the cubicle next to you. It comes from doing the work you love to do, that you were born to do—or having the freedom to experiment enough to find it. It comes from leaving money second on your priority list, after your gratification, which should always be your first priority. Pleasure is not a matter of getting married or staying single. It exists when you have the courage to establish yourself as a sensually free citizen. For one woman this may mean having many lovers. For another woman it may mean monogamy. For still another, it could be celibacy. You, my darlings, call the shots. Pleasure comes from giving yourself permission to explore your appetites freely, with no guilt.

Pleasure is about right here, right now. It is the spot you choose to be. Auntie Mame said, "Life is a banquet, and most dumb bastards are starving to death." Don't be a dumb bastard. Get thee to the banquet table. Your seat is waiting.

I'm advocating the lifelong investigation of pleasure, and this task requires all of your five senses. This is a new frontier for most people. We're trained to turn away from pleasure, to ignore pleasure, to abandon it, really. When you begin to investigate it, you feel you're being kind of naughty—or heading for trouble, like when you snuck out after curfew in high school. Like, "This feels really good, but it must be wrong, and there might be consequences." We usually need a big excuse to treat ourselves well—like a birthday. Imagine if you paid as much pleasurable attention to yourself every day as you do on your birthday. You might dress in your favorite outfit; give yourself a long, delightful bath; have exactly the food you want to have; go for walk, and shop in a store; meet up with some friends. What if we created a life where this was the rule, rather than the exception—where every day was about our pleasure, our passion, our fulfillment?

Sounds selfish, no? *No,* it's not. For true generosity does not occur unless you give from your own surplus. In other words, until you have yours, you don't have anything to give others. Some people can experience surplus when they have a dollar in their pocket. Some feel poverty when they have a million dollars. Our exploration of the womanly arts will be about which experiences, which circumstances lead to the creation of a truly fulfilled life.

You'll find that a pleasurable life requires constant vigilance. Stay true to what you want, listen to your instincts. For some of you this means allowing someone to touch you only when you want to be touched, and touching someone only when you want to. Or refusing to involve yourself in that trap of servicing others in the hope that they'll do something nice in return. Embracing pleasure is about looking within, to see what would feel good, and following through on any and all activities that can add to your own gratification. Sometimes your pleasure will come from declining an offer from someone else. Sometimes it comes from doing something simply for the joy of seeing that fulfilled look on another's face.

When a woman really begins to pay attention to her desires—ah, that is when the real pleasure begins! It is so much fun to want something. It is fun to move toward gratifying that want. It is even fun to change your mind. And it is so much fun to have others join you in the pursuit of your desires. It is a pleasure to be a woman enjoying her desires, and a pleasure to be around a woman enjoying her desires. Appetite drives the world. And when a woman feels great about what she wants—great about wanting, and confident that whatever she wants can and will be fulfilled—we all have a really good time.

Good things come to those who feel good. And any woman going for hers inspires us to go for ours. That is Mama's goal for the School of Womanly Arts—for women to inspire one another to move toward their best life by embracing the pursuit of pleasure, rather than the "No pain, no gain" philosophy. I consider my role in relationship to my Sister Goddesses as the fanner of the flames of their desires. We all want new possibilities, more pathways, to realize our dreams. With pleasure by our side and the Goddess at our back, we can create lives that are rewarding and rich on every level.

Real independence, self-knowledge, courage, and determination are required to attain our deep, true craving, since we are the only ones who can identify them and no one else is really much interested in whether they come to fruition or not. It is a solo journey, my beauties! But now Mama is here to help set you on that path to pleasure; and in this culture, where pleasure does not top the priority list, we need all the flame fanning we can get.

The following are some guiding principles of Mama Gena's School of Womanly Arts. May they lead you to your land of desires, wishes, hopes, and dreams. We will be using them as a basis for all the lessons to come. Take note, darlings, and get ready for more fun and freedom than you might have thought possible.

Decide That Wherever You Are Is the Right Place to Be

A little secret I'm going to share with you here is that getting your bliss starts with finding the bliss WHERE YOU ARE. This is a key step. Many of us have trouble accepting the rightness of ourselves, but that's something that Goddess worshipers practiced for centuries. Only now, in the tiny smattering of time that is the last five thousand years of human existence, that we have grown to disapprove of our bodies, our essential selves.

But thousands upon thousands of people have put self-doubt, judgment, and self-loathing aside and are ready to get on with the business of becoming a Sister Goddess. And a key step in becoming a full-fledged S.G. is to party, rigorously, from where you are.

I had to find my own starting point on the way to Goddessdom. I had to find the perfection where I was—in the spot I had been telling myself for years was all wrong. You will take a monumental step if you can just see that the path to pleasure doesn't begin with a bop on the head from Mama Gena but begins with a decision, a simple decision that each of us must make: we merely must acknowledge that what we have is good now. Not "Life will be good, if only . . ." Not "Life would have been good, except . . ." No, my sweethearts, it is good now. You have had the genius to pick up this book, now, haven't you? And I wrote it at exactly the right moment, exactly the right time and place where our paths would cross. I did not write it a hundred years ago, so it would be out of print, or a hundred years from now, when you would be long gone. The time is now. The revolution is that you are my sister and you are a Goddess. I do not care if you clean toilets for a living or your husband beats you or you've never had an orgasm or you are blind or deaf or in a wheelchair. I don't care if you make millions and you hate yourself or you drink too much or you weigh three hundred pounds. You are my sister and you are a Goddess. As such, you have the power to create the existence you want, no matter how bleak a life you are currently living.

It requires the most inspiring kind of courage to accept that what you have is good. S.G. Helen, the daughter of therapist parents, spent her twenties blaming her parents for her lack of success in life, her lack of love, her lack of happiness. None of this blame ever led her to happiness. In fact, it led to more and more unhappiness. She hung out with other miserable people. When I first met her, she had just broken off with her best friend, a drug user to whom she had given thousands of dollars. She dragged her sorry ass to Mama Gena's, and the first thing she heard from us was: Celebrate and enjoy NOW. Don't wait for things to change. Look around for the perfection in your life as it exists, in this moment. See what you see. Of course, we want you to think about what you want, but that will come way quicker if you love now.

So S.G. Helen looked around her. Friendless, careerless, and boyfriendless. Seemed gloomy at first glance. She was not inclined to celebrate. She had no practice in looking for the good. She felt a bit crybabyish and misunderstood about the whole thing. She did not want to look for the good, thank you very much. She was attached to her misery. Then she woke up to something. She had practiced misery for a decade. She saw what it brought her, and was actually bored by it. It was time to try something new, no matter how scary or weird. It had to be better than more of the same old victimhood. So she glanced around with a new perspective.

She realized that she had survived the AIDS epidemic intact; that she had escaped the fate of so many people of her age, who were in the middle of messy divorces or child custody battles. She had no one demanding her time or money. She had her own apartment. She could come and go as she pleased. She was free, healthy, and up for adventure in the greatest city in the world. It was a week later that Helen met the guy who would eventually become her husband. I believe this is a natural consequence of her courageous choice to love herself and love her life. She stopped blaming her parents, herself, her friends. She stopped being a victim, not through endless years of therapy but after deciding to look for the perfection of her circumstance. It seems as though the Goddess is hovering in the periphery of our lives, just waiting for us to make the decision that life is good. As soon as we grab hold, she gives us the most unexpected kick up the ladder to our dreams. You start loving life; she provides the kick.

Love Your Flesh

Whenever I talk about accepting pleasure in your life, I'm reminded of a fabulous scene in Oprah Winfrey's genius movie, *Beloved.* Maybe you saw the movie or read the book by Toni Morrison. An older woman, a grandmother type named Baby Suggs, gathers all the freed slaves together in the beautiful woods. She exhorts the children to laugh, encourages the men to dance, and tells the women to cry. Baby Suggs helps those around her to accept all of themselves, to rediscover the range of emotions and life that they had been taught to repress as slaves. She holds her gnarled hand in the air and says, "Love your flesh!" Toni Morrison knows that freedom begins with the act of self-love, not the thought or the theory but the act.

In many ways, we still live in a culture that teaches us to hate our flesh and to devalue our physical existence. But we can and must teach ourselves to love our flesh. Love is self-protection. Love your flesh and you will take a very important step toward identifying and loving your vision of the world and of life as you want it to be. Until you love yourself you will never be free to love someone or be loved.

How do you start loving yourself silly? You know you have spots of your fine self that you just adore. We all do. Rather than focusing all of your attention on the parts of yourself that you disapprove of, simply find ways to celebrate your goodies. It causes them to multiply.

Sister Goddess G. Adrienne did just this when she came to her school of womanly arts graduation. Adrienne had been a yo-yo dieter her whole life. During her Mama Gena class, she agreed to stop dieting and just enjoy herself in her own skin for the extent of the class. The day before graduation, she took herself lingerie shopping and bought some sexy undies. The night of her graduation she was so carried away by her enjoyment of her own fine self that she flashed a room full of Goddesses her new sexy bra. She didn't realize until the next week that she had lost five pounds. Adrienne's celebration of her body—*not* dieting—had led to her weight loss. Celebrate yourself and revel in the rich and often unexpected rewards that come with that new mind-set!

Sister Goddess Sylvia altered her relationship with her body—and her boyfriend's relationship with her body—simply by changing her mind. After Sylvia moved in with Arthur, she put on a few pounds. Arthur noticed and told her she had a fat ass. At first Sylvia was upset, but after her Womanly Arts class, she returned home with a new attitude. We had her look in the mirror and pose, and appreciate her gorgeous, juicy butt. The very next day Arthur, who is a photographer, stopped her, midday, to ask her if he could photograph her butt in the beautiful afternoon light. Somehow his attitude had undergone a real transformation. She was delighted that her own attitude adjustment had such immediate consequences.

Remember to love your mind as well as your body. Approval makes us independent, strong, and wonderfully willful. For most of us, our margin self-confidence is often so slim that a drop of anyone else's disapproval sends us into the chute of negativity and self-doubt. Self-criticism keeps us weak and malleable, it allows us to give our power away to others.

So fling open your door to acknowledgment and approval and self-celebration. Blast S.G. Aretha Franklin singing "Natural Woman" or Helen Reddy singing "I Am Woman." Whoever your internal Diva is, let her remind you who you are. Even if all you did today was think about how you might spoil yourself, that is a step. Celebrate any clever thought that presents itself to you.

When Auntie Beth, my protégée, first came to work with Bruce and me, it took some work to get her into the mind-set. Every few days she would descend into a pit of self-disapproval. To counter her negativity, we would send her into our empty course room and have her dance naked and sing to some sexy, empowering tunes. After about twenty minutes of being outrageous, she would emerge, eyes sparkling, ready to party again. Do anything and everything you can think of to celebrate your unique beauty and increase your joy.

Pleasure is love. Love of yourself first, foremost, and always. This takes some discipline and work, but the rewards are ample. If you respond to the true call of self-love, you begin to live a life that gratifies you. You begin to live your life as you define it. And that, my darlings, is the first step in creating healthy, fun partnerships with people.

Take Your Daily Dose of Fun

Not long ago, I found myself in the doldrums. I had been working nonstop for two weeks and enjoying every second of it. But then came the day when the thought of sitting in my chair and working made my head explode. My husband, Bruce, suggested I go for a facial. I didn't want to, but I did. As soon as I was out of the house and heading to the salon, I felt better. By the end of the facial I felt fantastic. I was refreshed and ready for more fun, more work, more whatever. Bruce helped me get on the right track. I recommend having a fun partner who can help fill your days with such excellent energy, but if you don't, you have to pull yourself up by your own bootstraps, gals, and go for fun!

If you're being a good girl, working hard, and living up to your obligations, but clean living is just not making you happy—change and do something else. You are in a rut, a rut that's not for you, and you're wasting your time. If you are not having fun, you simply won't have enough energy to shift direction in life. The last thing in the world you will feel like doing when you are not having fun is . . . having fun. So don't let yourself sink so desperately low.

A woman in pursuit of a pleasurable life will maintain her sense of humor at all costs. Even Mother Nature has a killer sense of humor. A kangaroo is a hilarious invention. A penguin? Too hysterical. Each of us can add a little fun to our lives, even in small ways, and the result can be a hugely entertaining life. You can make the decision to take control of something awful and turn it into something funny.

S.G. Jill was riding in a car with her husband, David, on the New Jersey Turnpike, near New York City. Their children, Samantha and Thomas, were in the backseat. The traffic was bumper-to-bumper, moving just enough to be excruciating, and David was honking and cursing as a result. Temperatures were rising. At one point the average speed on the turnpike rose to about forty miles per hour, and a little distance grew between their car and the one in front of them. Looking to gain any bit of momentum, a van swerved in front of this Sister Goddess and her family's car, almost hitting them. Without thinking, S.G. Jill followed the first impulse she had: she sat up in her seat, pulled up her shirt, and flashed her breasts to the driver. The move was just the thing to break the tension in the car. Everyone in the car started laughing. S.G. Jill asked David if he felt better, and he did, delighted with his wife's outrageousness. Her spontaneous move changed the whole tenor of the day.

Maybe you would say S.G. Jill's actions and words were shocking. But be honest—how many times have you squelched the thought of doing something because you thought it was too outrageous? It's happened to us all. Well, it's time to let that restraint go. The wildness, the spontaneity that is you delights the universe. Release and you will be rewarded with your wishes, just like Aladdin with his lamp. But your wishes aren't limited to three—you get as many as you can dream!

The pursuit of pleasure should be exhilarating. And while it takes absolutely no effort to have a miserable life, building a glorious life is another matter. You have to reach for it. Sneaking in a little fun for yourself can be life altering and awe inspiring. I love to see the excitement and energy that emanates from Sister Goddesses in training when they truly let their desires loose. It is so invigorating to see them rediscover their desires and change not only their experience of life but the way all those around them experience the world.

Expose What You Truly Feel

Most of us have been taught to keep our truths to ourselves and to tell people what we think they want to hear, or what we think we *should* be feeling. We feel awkward about what we really want. Exposing what we want requires truth telling, even when it makes us feel uncomfortable. When you can share your desires with those around you, you are being truly yourself and you will find that you connect with the people you know and meet in a much stronger way. Sister Goddess Jenny was one of my pupils who discovered just how powerful telling the whole truth can be.

S.G. Jenny had a guy, Ron, in her life who was always trying to flirt with her and get close to her. So naturally she avoided Ron constantly. Finally Jenny got up the nerve to tell Ron she liked him as a friend but wasn't attracted to him. As it turns out, Ron was totally fine with that. Then guess what happened? Jenny actually began to like Ron more, and actually became attracted to him—which surprised and delighted them both. After a few months of being just friends, Jenny and Ron talked honestly again about what was going on between them and agreed to move their relationship into the romantic realm and start dating. You never can tell what will happen when you trust that truth you feel and let its power lead you.

Sister Goddess Krisztina had a similar experience with truth-telling. She came to New York, with her boyfriend, from Budapest. After a few months here, he went home; she decided to stay. S.G. Krisztina wanted what she wanted, and that was a life here, in this country. Being on her own in this new land was not what she had planned, but this Sister Goddess was not deterred. She stuck with her desire in spite of the unexpected obstacles she faced.

This outlook served S.G. Krisztina very well. She got a job, then met a new guy, another expatriate named Steve. They had this hot, fabulous affair for a few months. Somewhere in there, Steve had to move, and Krisztina invited him to move in with her. There was no formal agreement—it just kind of happened even though Steve felt he was too young for a steady girlfriend. Then things got serious: as neither one of them was a legal resident, they entered the green card lottery. They said they would get married if either of them won, in order to give the other a green card. This would be just a business transaction. When Steve won the green card lottery, however, he was reluctant to go through with it. Krisztina wanted him to buy her a ring and pressed him to marry her. This didn't make either of them feel good. She didn't feel wanted, and he felt pressured. Their relationship was a time bomb, ready to explode. When Krisztina popped into the school of Womanly Arts, Steve had left her and moved to Florida that morning.

Krisztina was desolate. She knew Steve loved her, too, but the more she tried to keep him, the faster he moved away from her. That was the key—Krisztina was spending her life trying to please Steve to gain his love or acceptance, which only backfired.

Mama put Krisztina in pleasure boot camp. She had to take candlelight baths, pamper herself, go out with her girlfriends (which she hadn't done in years!), and flirt with other guys. There is no quicker way than flirting for a woman to remember who she truly is. Suddenly, Krisztina's power came flooding back to her. She realized she was more than a hausfrau—she was a bright, beautiful, sexy young woman. She had been keeping a lid on her own fun for far too long, and blaming Steve for it. Krisztina actually felt grateful to Steve for leaving her—if he hadn't, she never would have signed up for the School of Womanly Arts and never found her way home.

Shortly after this epiphany, Krisztina and Steve talked. Krisztina told him she wanted him back. She said this straightforwardly, she didn't whine or complain. She called him as she soaked in her tub filled with bubbles and candles, and told him how much fun she was having. Krisztina's voice had a delicious, sexy, inviting quality that Steve hadn't heard before. He really wanted to be part of this world she was creating for herself.

Well, soon that boy became intoxicated. He began to call Krisztina every day, curious to hear the next installment of her whirlwind life. Six weeks later Steve was back in New York, and more in love with Krisztina than ever. He continues to call her every day when they are at their jobs, and they are having the most wonderful time of their lives.

S.G. Krisztina ended up getting the life *and* the man she wanted the most effective way possible—by making her very own path of pure pleasure toward them both. If you choose the pleasure path, as Krisztina did, you will soon discover that the universe and other people start responding to you in a very positive way. Your sparkling energy draws those things you desire toward you, and there is really nothing at all to push them away. Is it hard to understand why this approach is so effective? Wouldn't we all choose to spend our time with fulfilled, gratified, fun-loving people rather than with a bunch of whiners and complainers? When you accept the power of yourself and your pleasure, you will find that the habits of moaning and lamenting will fall away. They have no place in the life of a truly pleasured woman.

Be Responsible, Fulfill Your Desires

Living a glorious life is an option for those of us fortunate enough to live in America. You have the freedom to make your own life exactly the way you'd like it. Now go out and make it.

Arrange your career to suit your pleasure. Let S.G. Alessandra's actions inspire you. After months of endless pressure at a job in which she was asked to take on more responsibility and longer hours for no more pay, she got fed up. One day, Alessandra walked right into her boss's office and said, "If I don't have time to have sex with my boyfriend, eat dinner with my boyfriend, or go to the gym, I am not working here!" Instead of letting Alessandra go, her boss talked her into staying by meeting her desires with a raise and shorter hours. I wasn't surprised when I heard the news, but Alessandra sure was. Her boss's response to her requests was such a surprise, it changed her whole perspective on how she could live and what she could achieve. Next time, Alessandra says, she'll speak up for what she wants before things get ugly.

Alessandra's revelation can be a lesson for all women. The responsibility is ours to create a new playing field. But this is trickier than it seems. For just as we have been taught to exterminate our joy, we have to be taught to revive it. Like Alessandra, we must all have the guts to make that first move, to pick up the ball—and then we have to run with it. That's where I'm hoping this book is going to come in handy for you. When you are tentatively stepping out there to create your desired lifestyle, this can be your handbook of advice, inspiration, and ideas. It can bolster your courage and give you a variety of options and examples to follow as you plot your own path to eternal pleasure.

S.G. Alessandra could never have fixed her work situation if she hadn't been focused on her desire. It was Alessandra's unbridled lust that captured her boss's attention. This Sister Goddess would never have gotten the same response from him if she had played the part of the shy, retiring, hopeful subordinate. No, it was Alessandra's boldness, her courage to voice her desires fully and strongly, that got her what she wanted.

Follow Your Divine Intuition

We really are Sister Goddesses. Most people find the appellation "S.G." amusing and fun. It is. It is also the truth. But it also reminds us of an essential truth—as women, we all have a divine spark within us. It's our duty to respect that divinity, to follow our instincts and our feminine intuition.

If you learn to move from your enthusiasm or your lust, you will be doing so much for yourself. For example, if you kiss a guy only when you really want to, rather than when you feel you have to, you would really enjoy it. Or if you eat only what you really want, prepared exactly as you want it, in the most celebratory way, you would ultimately make the best choices. Glorifying the Goddess in you is all about paying true attention to what you desire each and every moment of the day, just as you would if you were the caretaker of a beautiful shrine. Treat yourself as the beautiful shrine that you are—whenever you get the chance, toss rose petals at your feet!

The more goddessly you become, the more offers of all kinds will come your way. Your only obligation is to use your instinct as your guide. It is OK to decline an offer, even if it is something wonderful, if you have had enough wonderful for the day.

Yesterday my husband, Bruce, sent me for a facial and bought me a new wallet and two beautiful pairs of earrings. We also took our daughter, Maggie, to an art opening. Bruce was enjoying all the fun we were having and was reveling in his generosity. He wanted to take us all out to dinner. I got caught up in the spirit of the day and agreed—even though I was getting a strong sense that I was too full from the richness of my day to be able to eat at my favorite restaurant that night. If I had listened to my intuition, which was whispering that she wanted to go home, I would have been on the right track. When we got to the restaurant, it turned out that there was an hour's wait for a table, and we ended up heading home. My intuition had told me an hour before that dinner wasn't going to be a go, but I did not speak her truth, so we all made an unnecessary trip. I know this is a small detail in life—getting a table—but I offer up this example just to illustrate how important and helpful it can be to stay tuned in to your inner truth and her wisdom at all times. I'm telling you, gals, she won't let you down!

Don't bother to deconstruct your intuition. Asking why is like trying to figure out a very complex puzzle, and its solution, if you happen upon it, is not always very interesting. My advice is that you take a pleasure reading of yourself (have you had enough fun today? this minute?) often and, based on what you find, just take appropriate action. Most of us get really hung up on the long, crooked, ungratifying trip into Why Things Are the Way They Are. This trip is usually a big maze with no cheese at the end. The problem with looking for the *why* of it all is that you never really, truly find it. And if you do, it doesn't necessarily make your life any better.

Sister Goddess Stacey was one who needed to forget about why. She had such intimacy issues that, as one of her former boyfriends said, she would have been best off dating an astronaut. By the time she came to Mama, it had been years since Stacey had had a relationship. In that time, she had become used to feeling guilty and wrong about her resistance to getting close with guys. After learning a few womanly arts, S.G. Stacey decided to do something different. Instead of wasting a lot of time trying to understand the psychological reason for her behavior, S.G. Stacey decided to just enjoy the time she spent with a new guy who had entered her life, and also to enjoy the time they were apart. Well, lo and behold, Stacey found that she enjoyed living her life much more than examining her intimacy issues. S.G. Stacey realized that, over time, she became more and more willing to accept her new man's attention. Then, one night, he gave Stacey the keys to his apartment. The old Stacey would have recoiled in fear at the intimacy of this key sharing, but the new S.G. Stacey was thrilled and excited by the progress they were making together.

All of us, even when we are doing exactly what we love, can momentarily focus too much attention on accomplishing the goal and forget to pay attention to our pleasure. That is the precise moment to take a break. Stress and burnout occur if you don't. Ecstasy returns to you if you do!

In order to inspire you to take the path of pleasure, I want to fill your head and your heart with tales of some women who are already on the path. Most of the old gals we've been brought up to emulate are gonna have to put on their walking shoes. They won't serve us now. Yes, the time has come to bury Snow White, Cinderella, Sleeping Beauty, and the Little Mermaid. It's time to rid yourself and your world of that passel of subservient, paralyzed, codependent, weak, passive, self-sacrificing, powerless role models. It's time to think Pippi

Longstocking style. Your brave new world is the world in which you make the rules, based on your pleasure. In this new world there are no limits to your power. I know this is a big new reality to embrace. Sometimes to start living this new way you have to act as if this is how you've always done things. Do whatever it takes to take that first step, and then all you'll have to do is keep the momentum going.

Some of the most empowered women I know are your Sister Goddesses. They may not be mythic yet, but they're legends in the making. These ladies have begun paving their own way to pleasure, first by embracing the sublime pleasure of the ridiculous. Consider following in their footsteps.

In one bragging session recently, a roomful of Goddesses and I listened to the typically private and retiring S.G. Hiroko recount an adventure. She went to visit some girlfriends in Rhode Island. She had just started her class and wanted to bring a little wildness to her chums. She talked them into skinny-dipping at midnight in a neighbor's pool, and they ended up having the kind of laugh these gals hadn't had in ages.

In another example of Sister Goddess silliness, S.G. Brenda, age fifty-six, single, dateless for years, decided to fire up her motor. She had an appointment for a haircut with her sexy hairdresser. She bought some new red satin undies and decided to wear them to the haircut. This was her little secret. The hairdresser went mysteriously wild over her, flirting and fussing for hours. S.G. Brenda began to feel the power of her panties, the power of her giving herself permission to flirt.

Are you noticing the trend? Pleasure definitely requires choosing fun over others' expectations, over obligations. When women realize that they don't have to be ashamed of their desires, you'd be amazed at how they can have their way. Follow your appetite, your desires, your secret wants. Do so, and your life will change for the better.

S.G. Sydney is an accomplished doctor with a naughty secret. She developed a flirtation with a male nurse at the hospital, and now discreetly sees him outside work. This adds a bit of swing to her step and enlivens her routine at work. Some people may not approve of Sydney's actions, but she and the boy toy feel great and always look forward to spending time at the hospital. I say that all signs indicate Sydney is making the right decision for herself—she feels great! Who cares what anybody else has to say about her extracurricular activities?

Now, people always talk about how you have to pay the piper. For every great experience, there's a disappointment. When you break up with someone, for instance, you have to go through that bottoming-out, mourning period, right? Wrong! Following your desires can make the good times better and minimize the bad times. S.G. Abby broke up with her boyfriend of many years and went on five dates during the following week. Two of her dates were with a songwriter she really likes, her idea of fun is to have him write songs about her. For Abby, partying is an alternative to months of grieving and recuperating over her ex.

S.G. Bette added a dose of fun to her life during a recent squabble with her husband. She and her husband are usually kind of quarrelsome, but this time, when Bette and her man started bickering, she refused to slide into the familiar ugly mood that usually overtook her. Instead, when emotions boiled over a bit, she put herself on a sensual diet: she took herself out for a Burberry plaid pedicure, did a little self-pleasuring and had sex with her husband five times in the same week. Every time they began to lock horns, she locked him in the bedroom. They had the best week of their lives.

Remember how I was saying that if you change your outlook and relationship to pleasure, you'll change the world for those around you? Well, from what I've witnessed, the first thing a rockin' and rollin' Sister Goddess wants to do is invite her pals along for some fun. For example, S.G. Maura took a trip to Saint Bart's and really cut loose—she sunbathed topless and dated all the cute waiters at the hotel. She'd never considered such a thing before. But now she realized she could have way more fun than she had ever thought, and the fact that she had all kinds of guys offering to buy her champagne and dinner was an added bonus. One man was so entranced by Maura and her pursuit of pleasure that he invited her to quit her job and sail to Spain with him. Maura didn't take Mr. Spain up on his offer, but she was delighted to receive it.

This was the best vacation S.G. Maura had ever had. But her favorite part of the trip was teaching her friend Nancy the knack of having fun, too. Now, Nancy was a generous gal who was always paying for herself and others. Maura showed her how irresistible a woman can be when she's enjoying herself—in her case it made every man in a one-mile radius want to offer her champagne. On the last night of their island getaway, Nancy came running over ecstatically to tell Maura that a guy bought her, not a glass, but a bottle of champagne. It looks to me as if after one short vacation, Maura is making a Sister Goddess out of Nancy. Sharing the fun seems to be the name of the game!

The pursuit of pleasure requires a willingness to reach for the good, no matter what the circumstance. It's only when you reach for it that you find it. You can even fake it till you make it. S.G. Meg was on a flight to Paris. The plane was stuck on the runway for three hours, then she was told it would not be taking off at all. She was furious. But it was week two of womanly arts training, and suddenly she thought, that she had learned "What would Mama say? She'd say that the fact this is happening to me is perfect, somehow, someway." Just as she uttered those words, she glanced up and noticed a really cute guy. They ended up having a drink together, then dinner, as they waited for a new flight. Meg had not been dating for a while (she was a bit gun-shy after a nasty breakup) and here she was being forced, against her will, to hang out with this adorable man for hours upon hours in an airport. They ended up being put on the same plane for the flight back to New York, and stayed up half the night talking. They exchanged numbers as they landed, and Meg was so thrilled. She decided the entire experience was a little gift for her, a reward for her willingness to accept the rightness of her situation.

* * *

This is my idea of a pleasurable life: Being with friends, sharing my life, enriching my child's life with influences beyond what my husband and I can provide—living in the company of other kids and adults. Living in the city and near the ocean. In a truly pleasurable life, I am contributing the parts that I enjoy doing, and other people cover the parts that I don't—like laundry, cleaning, cooking. Creating my business, with my husband partnering me in my vision, is pleasurable.

I have been in the process of inventing and reinventing my life, creating and re-creating my vision, for my whole life. In my experience, dedicating yourself to pleasure does not cause a bolt of lightning to change you overnight. It gradually aligns your thoughts and actions with what you desire. It is a journey that requires paying attention to what you want, and making mistakes that you learn from. If you find your path, as I found mine, you will learn what to hold on to and what to discard as time goes by. Pleasure encourages you to notice what lights you up—and what doesn't. Building your life around personal fulfillment requires that you choose what lights you up again and again, each and every day.

In real life, I don't live on the beach, nor do I live in a house full of friends. Someday I may. But while I do have bigger goals and aspirations that I am moving toward, I also have to acknowledge that what I do have is incredibly wonderful. I live in a big rented brownstone in New York. I have phenomenal next-door neighbors, whose kids are in and out of my house all the time. I work with Beth, my dear friend, and my beloved husband, Bruce, in our third-floor offices. I have fantastic, funny, creative friends who inspire me continually. I love the gang of rotating Goddesses who work with us, stay for dinner, gossip, and play with Maggie. In addition to the gaggle of Goddesses that wander in and out of the brownstone, there are others who come and go. My best friends from California come to stay and work with us for at least a month each year. I have the most adorable, funny, loving housekeeper, named Carmen, and the beautiful Marti, who takes exquisite care of my daughter. The most important element in my current life is the spirit of work and love and play and company that is present constantly. I love the people who surround me in my home.

So now we are going to shift the focus to *your* dreams and goals and wishes. Hopefully we have stimulated your imaginative juices to the degree that some deep desires are ready to surface. So, come on, gals, step up and be your full, free, fabulous selves! Consider this your formal invitation. Of course, it takes practice and some courage and eternal vigilance to embrace a great life. But there's no reason to hesitate a moment longer. Get the fun started with these exercises I've designed to help you flex your freedom muscles. Make the fun workout part of your daily schedule.

We are about to move into the how-to section of this lesson. You may wonder why. The reason, oh my divine darlings, is that y'all have such bad habits. Mama wants a shot at retooling. These exercises don't require a lot of preparation or material. They are activities that will help you to get in touch with your self and your appetites. The fastest way to Sister Goddessdom is to do all the exercises—the women in my courses who do every drop of homework have the most glorious results. Even if they are uncomfortable with the exercises, even if they are skeptical, magnificent results happen anyway. You may resist these exercises. Some of them may even seem silly to you, or maybe you think you don't need the practice. But in my experience, we can all use the practice.

Exercise 1: The Forecast

Most of us don't notice how we disapprove of ourselves constantly. We run this continuous doubt tape in our heads, which says, "This is wrong," "That's the wrong thing to say," "This could be better," "That's too much food," "That's too much money," "That's not a good job," and so on. It's good to add on some approval, some positive reinforcement. Decide that you are always, on some level, responding exactly the right way to whatever is happening. Notice your genius and approve of it.

Check in with yourself regularly, perhaps every hour for an entire day. Identify exactly how you feel in that moment—happy, sad, frustrated, envious, exhausted, sullen, whatever. Write it down. Each time you do, say the following phrase: "I'm __________ and that is a right way to feel." Fill in the blank. Celebrate whatever is happening, even a change in weather, and how you feel about it.

Exercise 2: Thank-You Notes

Being grateful is healthy for many reasons. First and foremost, it feels wonderful. Second, when you begin to notice the good you have in your life, you open yourself up to more good. You create space. Third, when you concentrate on being thankful, you begin to notice how many of your desires have actually come true.

Put together a "grateful" list: what are you grateful for? This practice will help you make a habit of the positive, deliberate act of thankfulness.

Exercise 3: The Ties That Bind

Make a list of all your beliefs, all of your cultural conditioning, all your unwritten rules about how women should behave. Take stock of how you're *supposed* to behave at work, among your peers, in a relationship. Your list might include things such as "I'm not supposed to sleep with someone on the first date," or "I shouldn't take a day off from work unless I'm sick," or "If I'm over thirty I should be married."

When listing your beliefs, you shed light on your long-held assumptions. What you see may surprise you. Notice how we just presume that God is male, or that someday our prince will come, or that we have to work to exhaustion to get what we want. Do you assume that to be married you have to choose between money and doing what you love, or that you have to be a Stepford wife? Do you feel you will never be rich? Or never find a life partner? Do you feel other people always get the breaks, and not you? Does motherhood mean slavery? Make this list and put it in a drawer. Pull it out a month or two after you finish this book. See if any of your past beliefs have fallen by the wayside.

I used to think that someday my prince would come. What I found out was that I could find a perfectly reasonable guy and turn him into my prince by communicating my desires to him, and appreciating him. Had I not recognized my belief and then changed it to suit my pleasure, I surely would not have the great partner and father of my little girl that I do today.

Exercise 4: The Womantra

A womantra is your statement about who you are, as a free woman on the planet, having your way. Here are some great examples of womantras that I love:

I am beautiful,
I am rich, and
I have everything I want.
Thank you, Goddess.

The earth is mine for the taking.
No more cooking, cleaning, or baking
Unless I want to, unless I want to.
Sex is for my satisfaction.
Give me a guy who can give me some action.
I always want to, unless I don't want to.

Freedom is new. Freedom is mine.
Freedom is absolutely divine.
Freedom is here. Freedom is now.
Freedom is the cat's meow.

Create your own womantra, your own personal statement of yourself as a woman. The benefits come not from dwelling on inequality but, instead, from fully experiencing your freedom. Just take your pen to paper and see what flows. Womantras don't have to rhyme. They don't have to make sense. They are for yourself just to entertain you and inspire you.

Lesson 2

The Womanly Art of Whetting Your Own Appetite

Oh let us dwell, let us revel for eternity, in the desires of women!

—Mama Gena

I can remember, at the age of six, being infuriated by the two-cookie limit my parents placed on my bedtime snack. To exact revenge and get my way, I stuffed my panties full of cookies, front and back (Burry's chocolate sandwich cookies, I recall), and as I leaned over to kiss Mums and Dadums good night, I hoped they wouldn't notice my midriff bulge. What a feeding frenzy lay ahead!

I can recall that I had no trouble polishing off my panty load. In fact, the sneak-and-eat method was so effective that I can recall many other versions of this game—hiding in the pantry, pulling frozen Tastykakes out of the freezer, sneaking down to the kitchen late at night and sitting cross-legged on top of the dishwasher, feeling the comforting whir and warmth as I munched. It is a wonder that I am not the size of a sumo wrestler. But if my appetite was the wrong size (as I was convinced it was), then how could I enjoy my desires in the company of others? You can't expose what shames you.

It has taken me a lifetime to find my way to trusting my appetite. There was trial, there was error. I learned from my mistakes as much as my triumphs. Every time I dug down and followed my bliss, it led to the most fantastical adventures. When I sucked it in and compromised my true desires, I was stuck.

֍ ֍ ֍

What happens to you when a guy asks you, "What would you like to do tonight?" Do you offer countless fabulous options that would thrill you—naked lobster dinner by candlelight, front row at the circus, tango dancing with a rose in your teeth? Do you hold back, waiting for his cue—"Whatever you want, dear"? Do you suggest something safe that you know won't offend him—dinner and a movie, or, "We could just stay home and rent a video. I'll cook"?

These last few ideas crop up far too often to be true yearnings. They are simply our default options. They're what we women suggest when we don't dare say what we really want, or don't know what our hearts desire. Audre Lorde put her finger on this problem we women have when she wrote, in *The Uses of the Erotic: The Erotic as Power,* "We have been raised to fear the 'yes' within ourselves, our deepest cravings." When a woman ignores her wants, they atrophy and disappear.

A client of mine, S.G. Leslie, lives on a fat trust fund. She, therefore, is the "breadwinner" in the family—yet she has created her life to totally revolve around her actor husband's job and lifestyle. They move when he gets work, not when she desires. Although she could afford full-time help and child care, she wears herself out washing and cooking and cleaning for the three kids. Despite her resources, Leslie cannot use what she has because she is so deeply invested in the traditional idea of what a woman is. She has lost touch with a deep, powerful truth—that her pleasure has value and plays a crucial role in her life and the life of her family.

Millions of women are like Leslie, so wrapped up in what they *should* want that they don't know what they actually *do* want. If you grew up in a cave, you would never miss the sun. You just wouldn't think about it—you would live your life in darkness, never knowing light was an option. In fact, if someone dragged you to the light, you would probably be offended and uncomfortable—"Like, who needs *this*? I was doing just fine in my cave!"

We women often can't tell what we want because we are taught never to give our wishes any time, energy, or priority. Guys don't really understand this. If I ask my husband if he wants something, he's got an answer right away, no inner conflict. In our culture, men are usually brought up to feel right about themselves, about what they want. They are taught to identify and pursue their dreams. But women don't know how to call forth their desires, and when they do appear, they don't know how to recognize or voice them. Those of us with truly deeply buried appetites actually get mad when someone asks us what we want. Have you ever overheard a conversation like this:

He says:	Where would you like to go for dinner?
She says (or just quietly fumes):	Why are you asking ME? Why don't you already know? Why don't you just TAKE ME SOMEWHERE THAT I WANT TO BE!!!
He's like:	Sor-ry!!! (as he wonders for the thousandth time what women really want, and how the hell he's supposed to figure it out).

Her angry response is just the current of unspoken desire finding its way out in frustration and anger.

Another consequence of denying our appetites instead of celebrating them is that our appetites turn against us. We overeat, overmedicate, abuse alcohol, or engage in other addictive behaviors. It is really no surprise that we have an epidemic of overweight women in this country. When women find an appetite they can express in a socially acceptable way, they go wild. Check out bulimia, anorexia—not exactly male problems, now, are they? Sure are an appetite thing, though.

The fascinating thing is that when we recognize and fan the flame of our true desire, not only do we greatly increase our chances of getting what we want, but our aberrant behaviors fall away as well. You are out to dinner with a new guy. You are having a nice time, but this is a first date, so you are not ready to let your guard down all the way. He says, "How about some dessert?" You are aching for a bite of the chocolate mousse cake with fresh whipped cream, but you don't want him to think you might get fat someday, or that you are an expensive date, so you politely decline. Especially since he wasn't going to have dessert himself. You leave the restaurant craving chocolate. He takes you home. You kiss him on the cheek, he leaves, you spy out the window, and as soon as he's in a cab, you rush to the corner deli and get a pint of chocolate chocolate chip ice cream. You end up feeling a little dissatisfied with the whole evening (and a little sick from devouring that whole pint of ice cream). And all you wanted was one little bite of chocolate cake. In fact, if you had allowed the guy to buy you the cake, you would have satisfied your desire, allowed him to spoil you, and you both would have enjoyed the date a whole lot more. So, our project is not to reinvent our hot, throbbing appetites, but simply to get in touch with them. You may not think you have any unfulfilled desires, but listen closely, dear sisters. They're only a whisper away.

The first thing that may happen when you start thinking about what you want is that you draw a complete blank. Fear not, my dears. This is only Lesson 2. If this happens to you, just make something up. Even if it's not exactly a burning desire, it is the first spark of the bonfire. It is you opening the cap of your genie bottle and letting that first burst of desire free. The more practice you have, the more your authentic appetite will erupt.

For example, S.G. Camille was walking around whining all the time that she didn't have a boyfriend and she wanted a boyfriend and no guys liked her and she would never get married. One day in class, we had her play a game—"What if you really liked being single?" we asked her. "Just pretend. What if there was no rush to be married? What if you actually enjoyed the way it is *now*?" S.G. Camille did not really like the idea, but she was willing to play along. As she did, she began to notice that she loved her autonomy. She thoroughly enjoyed fixing up her apartment exactly the way she liked it. She treasured being able to go out with her girlfriends or on dates, and not having to answer to anyone. She noticed she actually liked having something to complain about. S.G. Camille realized she had adopted this stance that life was wrong without a guy not because she believed it but because it had become a way to connect with her girlfriends.

S.G. Camille decided to act for a weekend as if what she had was what she wanted. She went to a party and enjoyed herself thoroughly. For one night, she gave herself permission to be deliberately single, and fabulous. She was probably the only woman in the room who wasn't doubting herself or trying too hard. Wouldn't you know, she met a guy at the party. He practically tripped over himself to get her number. After all, a woman in love with herself is a rare and intoxicating sight. Sister Goddess Camille agreed to go out with him and they had an amazing time. She was amused to discover that the guy she hooked lived in Chicago, not New York, and he was heading back home the next day. Her appetite had located the perfect man for a woman who was not interested in a relationship—he lived more than 500 miles away. He agreed to call her next month when he was back in town, and Sister Goddess Camille decided that was perfect—not a moment too soon.

We should banish our custom of deciding what we have is wrong. For it diminishes us and our power, creates wrinkles, discomfort, loss of power, loss of appetite, and paralyzes our ability to get what we want. Surrendering to what you have and trusting that it is what you want now creates an opening for more to rush your way with unimaginable velocity. Encouraging appetite is like a dance—the dance between loving what you have and living for what you want. It takes a willingness to believe, to know, or at least to pretend that you are on your way to getting everything your heart desires, and as author Florence Scovel Shinn says, it will come "under grace, and in perfect ways."

Part of a woman's rapport with her desires comes from her willingness to wallow in them. We don't have too many opportunities to explore our desires alone or in the company of other women. So make your own opportunities.

In class, one of the first assignments is to create a desire list. This is fun to do while curled up on the couch with a cup of tea, or at the office during a break in your day. Write down everything you want, from the tiniest desire (a good night's sleep) to the most lavish (a château in France). Try grabbing a girlfriend or two and share your desires with one another. It's a wonderful thing. Your desires will inspire each one of you to go for more and more, like fuel to the fire.

In fact, creating your own Sister Goddess network can be incredibly important to you on your trip to happiness. A group of Sister Goddesses (or even just one or two) can help you with another assignment, something called "bragging." We do this every week in class. Each woman has to brag about something wonderful that happened to her during the week. The benefits of this exercise are many. Each S.G. begins to acknowledge what's already good about her life. She becomes more comfortable talking about her desires and experiencing their fulfillment. And her bragging will inevitably inspire other women to go for more than they would on their own.

S.G. Doris, for instance, was writing an article for a magazine that she loved. As she turned in her article, she told the editorial director that she wanted to schedule a meeting with him to talk about creating a position for her as a contributing editor. He agreed! This ballsy move inspired Stephanie to take her design portfolio to a famous Madison Avenue designer that she had always wanted to work for and ask for a job. She realized she did not have to wait for an opportunity, she could create one.

We inspire one another by sharing the good things in our lives. One woman's step up the ladder of fun encourages everyone behind her to take a step up, too. Form a group of friends with whom to share desires and weekly brags. It will be your own circle of inspiration.

There are certain requirements, rules, and regulations for a successful bragging group. The participants must be kept on a rigorous diet of *bragging only*—no complaining, no put-downs, no comparing of oneself to others, and no qualifying or criticizing one's own brag. Your brag is perfect just as it is, even if it's just that you took a break and bought yourself a cappuccino on a hard day. Other members of the bragging circle have to be on the lookout for the gals who can't resist criticizing themselves. Stop those gals in their tracks and ask them to celebrate themselves instead.

One of the achievements of my School of Womanly Arts I am most proud of is its extended Sister Goddess community—of which you are now a member. One of the glorious benefits of becoming a Sister Goddess is sensing the sisterhood that exists among women and knowing that you can use our shared strength for your own benefit. It is so inspiring to see women encourage one another's creativity, confidence, enthusiasm. Women have so much to contribute to one another. So many have been in the spot you're in now and can point you in the right direction. When my older S.G.'s talk about menopause, for example, the younger ones benefit from their experience. When the younger S.G.'s talk about flirting, the older ones get inspired to see if their equipment still works. Which, of course, it does.

The support that an energized group of women can give one another is truly amazing. I've seen the outpourings of generosity in my classes time and again. Once, S.G. Meryl came into class and described how, while going for her dream, she found herself temporarily broke, and she was scared. That night, three of her Sister Goddesses quietly donated some cash to get Meryl over the hump. We have supported one another through cases of breast cancer, loss of parents, appendicitis, childbirth, breakups, marriages, divorces, and engagements. The S.G.'s kick one another in the butt when someone is getting lazy, like settling for a job they don't really want. They inspire one another to try harder and squeeze more joy out of every situation.

Of course, this kind of community lives on outside the classroom (or living room) as well. For example, S.G. Daphne is really great at getting hotel upgrades. No one does it better. She can be booked in the tiniest corner room and end up in the presidential suite at no additional charge. S.G. Margaret wanted some of that. She travels a lot and feels she gets the worst rooms, on the ground floor, even when she pays top dollar. She and Daphne went to Boston for the weekend. They stayed at the Copley Plaza on one of their special discount-package rates. Daphne went to work on the front desk. She was strong and sure, and very flirtatious. No waffling. "I bet you could do better than that—not that you have to," she said. S.G. Margaret caught her moves, and the next time she traveled, she got her first upgrade!

With or without your own Goddess network, of course, the time will come when you have to take your appetite out on the road alone. It will require some bravery and faith to stick by your desires. S.G. Jillian is another of my gals who followed her inner desires even when they dictated moves that at first didn't seem wise. S.G. Jillian's big dream was to have a show in New York. At one point this budding painter said no to an offer to exhibit her works at an art fair in Europe. Jillian did this to keep her focus just on New York. Everyone advised Jillian to take the chance to hang her work—anywhere—but she turned down the European art fair with no other prospects on the horizon. A month later, Jillian was out to dinner with her boyfriend and ran into some influential people from the New York art scene and was offered a solo show at a prestigious Madison Avenue gallery. Ask and you shall receive, says Mama!

Had Jillian accepted the offer to go across the Atlantic to the art fair, she would have been in Europe at the time she was asked to show her work in New York. It took courage for Jillian to say no to what was offered and cling to the power of her desires. But she did it, and those who do the same find that following their true desires works wonders for them—every time.

It's easy to be swayed by people who tell you that what you want can never happen. You may have to struggle to lose the sense that what you yearn for is wrong, sinful, unjustly selfish, or just plain bad. Before we take pride in our desires—the very things that define us—most of us are embarrassed and humiliated by them.

Mama will introduce you to some exercises and activities to get in touch with your genuine appetite and all the power that comes with it. You'll learn that surrendering to your true desires is as elevating and enriching as a walk on the beach at sunset. Ignoring your desires and giving in to societal standards is the equivalent of being stuck in bumper-to-bumper traffic on the Long Island Expressway at rush hour. With this book as your guide, you're gonna be spending way more time at the beach.

Exercise 1: How Attuned Are You to Your Appetite?

This exercise is designed to help you assess how freely your appetites are flowing, and how often you recognize and go after what you are truly hungry for. Read the following questions and pick A, B, or C. Then read on to score your appetite awareness.

1. If I were out to dinner on a date with a new guy

   A. I would do a Scarlett O'Hara—eat at home first, so I could order a salad and water and therefore appear delicate and easy to maintain.

   B. I would look at the menu, check out the prices, and order a midrange pasta dish so as not to press his budget.

C. I would give in to myself and order both the appetizers I want, the lobster entrée, and have a bite of all three desserts that tickle my fancy.

2. When someone asks me what I want for a gift

A. My mind goes blank and I stare like a deer caught in the headlights.

B. I leave it up to the giver and say, "Whatever you think."

C. I flash them my desire list and take them by the hand to Tiffany's to point out my favorite things.

3. When I think about my job

A. I am close to tears. It's not that I am just indifferent, or uninterested in what I am doing. I despair of ever finding something I like.

B. It's a way to pay the bills until I figure out what I want.

C. I am so grateful and thrilled to be doing what I am doing that I would actually *pay* to do what I am being paid for.

If you chose A: You are an appetitophobic. There's no amount of "too little" that you won't accept. No S.G. can subsist on this diet.

If you chose B: You suspect there may be more to life and yet you don't know how to go for it without appearing vulgar.

If C was your choice: You understand that the greatest gift you can give the world is a gratified *you.* You are a true Sister Goddess!

Exercise 2: Bragging

Bragging about the goodness in your life, especially your pleasurable accomplishments, unearths your desires and fans the flames of desire in other women. Yo' mama says you can never brag too much, and if you are like many women, you aren't bragging nearly enough. This exercise will help you introduce bragging into your womanly repertoire.

The idea is to look at your life and choose something you feel good about, and share it with a friend. Encourage her to do the same with you. You can brag about the fact that you took a moment in the midst of your busy day to get a manicure or stop for a cappuccino. Or maybe you were brilliant at a sales meeting or you flirted outrageously with your plumber. One of my S.G.'s once bragged that she got an airline to hold her plane for her while she purchased some erotica to read on the flight. Another one passed the bar and graduated magna cum laude from law school in the same week. As you share your accomplishments big and small, you will inspire one another. One of my Goddesses had amazing sex with her husband after a six-month hiatus, which inspired two other Goddesses to go for similar nights of matrimonial lust with their husbands. We can drive one another to heights unknown with consistent bragging. Doing this exercise on a daily or weekly basis will deliver the best results. In talking about the good, more good can come your way. This is a great way to support and expand true appetite.

Exercise 3: Spring Cleaning

You will want to do this exercise frequently to clean your mental closet of all the dust balls, lint, and collected crap from a lifetime of unfulfilled dreams and desires. When you don't clean out your closet—in other words, rid yourself of all the clothes that no longer fit, the stuff bought on sale that never got worn, the old favorites that are too worn out to be seen in public—there is no room for new goodies. In fact, with an overstuffed closet you may lose your desire to shop because you don't have a vacant spot to put anything new. You might even have quite lovely things that you have forgotten about. Or things that were once lovely but are now ruined by neglect. This exercise clears your mind of all that old yucky stuff so it can be open and receptive to new desires. You can do this exercise alone—to a wall—with a partner, or with a small group of friends. Follow these directions and you'll start your Goddess training with a clean slate on which to note all your newly recognized desires and appetites.

Spring Cleaning, Alone

An S.G. sits by herself and does this process aloud. She questions herself and then answers herself.

For example:

S.G. asks: What do you have on "desire"? (This question is always the same, and asked in a simple, expressionless way.)
S.G. answers: I have no idea what I desire.
S.G. asks: What do you have on "desire"?
S.G. answers: I remember when I was three and I desired a pink ribbon for my hair and my mother criticized me.
S.G. asks: What do you have on "desire"?
S.G. answers: I want a chocolate-covered pretzel right *now.*

Spring Cleaning, with a Partner (the Best Way to Do This Exercise)

You both should first agree to keep what is said in this exercise confidential so that you can be free in revealing your desires. Then sit facing each other, either at a café or some private place. One S.G. asks the other the same question, over and over for fifteen minutes. The other S.G. answers. Then they switch.

For example:

S.G. 1: What do you have on "desire"?
S.G. 2: I feel that I want my boyfriend more than he wants me.
S.G. 1: Thank you.
S.G. 1: What do you have on "desire"?
S.G. 2: When we were together last night he refused to have sex with me.
S.G. 1: Thank you.
S.G. 1: What do you have on "desire"?
S.G. 2: I love my new pink shoes I bought today.
S.G. 1: Thank you.

Spring Cleaning, with a Group

When three or more Sister Goddesses participate in this exercise, one of the S.G.'s agrees to be the monitor. She goes around the room asking each goddess, "What do you have on 'desire'?" At the conclusion of the exercise, another S.G. might return the favor and monitor for her. Do the exercise for at least twenty minutes. You will feel free and fabulously energized when everyone has cleaned her closet.

Exercise 4: A Desire List

In my classes I have every S.G. create a detailed desire list. Now it is your turn. It's simple. Get out a piece of paper and a pen. Put on your list anything your little heart desires—from pink pajamas to a back massage, a helicopter ride, a walk on the beach, sex on the beach, getting married (or divorced), being a star, having an orgasm, eating a chocolate ice cream cone—anything, anything, anything you want, minuscule to vast.

Once you've finished your list (for now), I recommend posting it in a prominent place—like the refrigerator or the door to your bedroom. That way other people can see what you want and bring things to you.

Check your list and update it once a month. Whenever you get something on your list write, "Thank you, __________," to whoever was responsible for giving it to you. You will be surprised how quickly your wishes become fulfilled!

* * *

Our desires are the best things about us. Surrendering to them gives each of us access to a life of endless adventure, possibility, and expanding joy. The absence of appetite is the absence of life itself. In order to become a true Sister Goddess, you must be able to recognize and celebrate your appetite. Hopefully, Lesson 2 has helped you begin to recognize your desires more clearly. The next lesson will give you the ability to fuel and expand your desires for a lifetime.

Lesson 3

The Womanly Art of Having Fun, No Matter What

An inordinate passion for pleasure is the secret of remaining young.
—Oscar Wilde

Now that we have established the fabulous importance of your appetites, it is time to create fertile ground in which to nurture them. Desires are encouraged by glee and reckless abandon. Any activity done with sheer exuberance increases your appetite for happiness. My job, as a sister and a Goddess, is to interfere with your doldrums. I want to help you put large obstacles in your boring day so you trip over them and remember the saucy gal you truly are. I want you to insert pleasure and mayhem into your routine just to see what shakes loose. Mama's gonna show you how to take out the good china and serve yourself on a silver platter whether you're at work or at home. Make a little mischief with me. I promise, it won't hurt. And it's for a really good cause.

If you are reading all of this and thinking that you've completely forgotten how to have fun, or are hard pressed to think of more than one thing in life that brings you pleasure, don't worry. Most of my S.G.'s are kind of hungry, or really starving, for fun when they cross Mama's threshold. My purpose in the time we spend together is to stuff my gals with fun—to force them (against their will, sometimes) to have way more pleasure than they thought possible, to indulge in way more fun than they think they deserve.

I know most of you gals out there have been subsisting on a diet of stale bread and water (in the fun/pleasure department), too, and are wondering why you feel a little wan, a little listless, a little less than ecstatic. Nothing like a little malnutrition to take the rosy glow out of an S.G.'s cheek. What happens when my gals start to indulge (which actually is no indulgence at all—it is a minimum daily requirement) is that they get something I call "glow." They begin to look, well . . . better. Dewy, somehow. You know the look I mean—when you have just had an amazing sensual encounter and you are wearing jeans and a T-shirt and no makeup and maybe your hair isn't even combed, but you look gorgeous and feel fantastic and everyone can tell. My S.G.'s get glow. You will get glow. But only if you pay attention to your joy.

Pleasure and fun (and I use those words interchangeably) are the secret to a gratified life, but using them is an art, one that we have been taught to ignore. We have been conditioned to believe that if we look good and work hard, we will find fun and pleasure. Ha!

Mama wants to help you go against your conditioning and start paying attention to your instinct, like a salmon swimming upstream to lay eggs. Mama wants to teach you the art of adding pleasure to your day. You will give yourself glow if you do. You will be a woman amongst women, noticed for her aura, her clarity, and her flair. Glow creates beauty in women of all ages, all body types, all backgrounds. Glow is the thing that people who go for face-lifts and tummy tucks and implants all want, but never get, from a visit to the surgeon's office. Glow comes from internal approval, not disapproval. Pleasure and fun create the environment where self-esteem and self-worship flourish.

☼ ☼ ☼

You want glow—you gotta have fun. That's the simple equation, my beauties. While working hard is great, hard work without fun is empty and meaningless. And fun is not all "Ha-ha, whee!" It is whatever experience entertains and grabs you. Sometimes fun is going to a movie that is so sad it makes you sob like a baby. I rent *Il Postino* or *Once Around* when I want that kind of fun. Fun can be doing volunteer work at an old folks' home. It can be allotting enough time to go to a museum and sit in reverence of your favorite painting for as long as you want. It could be running the marathon or, for some of us, watching the marathon. Fun could be trying on new clothes, or having a difficult but important talk with a friend. Listening to music. Eating exactly what you want. You get the idea—fun is yours to define anyway you like. You can give it a new definition every day of the week if it pleases you.

Most of us are in the habit of not having fun and not focusing on pleasure. But we can change our focus. We can begin to make pleasure one of our goals. Sound simple? The short answer is NO, it is not simple. It's simple to identify the goal, perhaps—but to redesign your life so pleasure and fun come first is earthshakingly difficult. Mark Twain said, "You can't throw a habit out the window. You have to walk it gently down the stairs." This is the reason why my School of Womanly Arts is a seven-week course—to ease each S.G. in training into dropping the habit of self-denial and making pleasure and fun priorities in her life. As you read this book, give yourself the same amount of time, or longer if need be. Don't be impatient. Allow yourself some space to change. Pleasure is a habit, just like working oneself to the bone is a habit. Remember, any habit, good or bad, takes time and effort to change.

If you want a life of glory, adventure, and daring, head into the uncharted territory called fun and pleasure slowly. Leave work a little early to take a class you want to take, or meet a friend for a quick drink. Put fresh flowers on your desk, take a break and buy a coffee for yourself and a coworker. Go out on your lunch break to shop, go to the gym, or get a manicure. Sit in the park and read a book while you eat a sandwich. Listen to music to inspire yourself. Have tea in a bone china cup. First and foremost, entertain yourself.

Be prepared—you will be criticized for enjoying yourself. But take heart, you won't be the first. Mae West ended up in jail after writing and performing her play called *Sex.* Ingrid Bergman was thrown out of Hollywood for her affair with Roberto Rossellini. Picasso, in his constant re-creation of himself, was widely criticized by the art community for his first Cubist painting. The critics thought Picasso had lost his mind, but he was just following what was in his heart. Follow your own inner desires, and who knows—maybe you will start a movement that will be remembered long after you're gone!

You don't have to get caught up in what the outcome is going to be—just use fun to chart your course, and you're sure to find yourself on your most daring adventure. To help you, I've come up with some exercises (at the end of this lesson) that can keep you on track and support you on your voyage. As you embark on your pleasure cruise, know that it is possible to become as well versed in what pleasures you as in what pains and disappoints you. All that following your pleasure requires is a little practice.

Let's start practicing at work. Many of us spend our whole life doing the things that are supposed to lead us to a great time but that actually lead only to more work, aging, stress, and exhaustion. If you doubt me, answer me this: is there ever a spot in your workday when your boss comes up to you and says, "Great job! Why don't you leave early and get a facial and a full-body massage?" Didn't think so. Not to mention that even if our bosses did say this amazing thing and we cut out on our jobs for a few hours in the middle of the day, we would feel guilty. C'mon, admit it! But I guarantee you—if you did break up your day with a facial and full-body massage, you would do a better job at work. You would feel pampered and radiant and refreshed—like a Goddess—and you would return to work with a clear head and an eager mind. But the way our work life is now, most of you would have to lie to take a pampering break in the middle of your day, despite the fact that everyone would benefit from such indulgence on your part. Yes, it sure seems like we have a lot of encouragement to work through lunch, work late, work weekends, and not much encouragement to go off and have fun or do nothing for a while. This is the way life is, in spite of the fact that you all know that you get your best ideas when you are on vacation. Am I right, or am I right?

We were weaned on pain, not pleasure. No wonder you feel guilty if you stay at home all day and lie in bed eating bonbons. In our culture, you are supposed to be in bed only if you are sick. We feel guilty and weird if we have too much fun because we are just not used to it. It's way easier to talk to your boss at work about the bad flu you just had, not so easy to discuss your latest sexploits with your boyfriend. And we all know which is *much* more fun.

We can resist pleasure so effectively because most of us have this odd little interior voice that says if we work hard enough, we will get pleasure someday. The "No pain, no gain" theory. We seem to expect that if we work hard enough, a good fairy is going to bonk us on the head someday and say, "Break time, sister! Take a week off at the spa of your choice! You've earned it, you deserve it!" My darlings, you will up and die (or faint, anyway) before the break-time fairy bonks you. We each have to assume a Goddess's crown, take her wand, and be our own break-time fairy.

I want you to assess your own break time. According to a survey by Expedia.com, 50 percent of American workers said they skipped vacation time because they were "too busy to get away." The study suggests that we have failed to use more than $19.3 billion worth of vacation time—about $200 for every working American! Can you believe it? No wonder people are overworked, overstressed, and burned out. We've even passed Japan in hours worked. The truth is that both hard work and following your bliss lead to success, but when your aim is pleasing yourself and having fun, success always follows. When you go for success and leave out pleasure on the way, your chances of enjoying life drop to fifty-fifty. Don't you want to better your odds for a happy life? I have seen many women do just that. You could join them—the choice is yours.

Take the example of S.G. Patricia, a lawyer. She liked what she did, but she had gotten into the habit of working her butt off at her very successful law practice. Lately she was beginning to get a little wan, worn out, and uninspired—she was feeling sapped by the needs of her clients and would have loved a visit from the break-time fairy. But

Patricia's job philosophy was to put her clients' needs first, always. She was surprised to discover what happened when she considered her pleasure and enjoyment as well as theirs.

When she began her Goddess training, Patricia started learning the techniques of inserting her fun quota into her usual all-work equation. She vowed to do one pleasurable thing for herself a day. Once she got the hang of it, Patricia was on a roll. Nothing could stop her and her quest for self-gratification. She bought herself a new hair clip, got a more comfortable chair, took a trip to a bookstore to browse during her lunch break. She also took more control over when meetings began and ended, to make sure they fit well into her schedule, not just those of her clients. Patricia began ordering in muffins and cappuccinos for everyone to make her office meetings more fun. Some days she'd even sneak in a workout at the gym during her lunch break. She wore sexier clothes and red heels, just to entertain herself. Outside of work, Patricia began planning enjoyable activities—dinner with a friend, a movie, a visit to a museum. She also found the time to fulfill a lifelong dream to become a Big Sister and mentor a child. Soon Patricia's days centered around her pleasurable experiences, with her clients' needs tucked in around them—she had pulled a complete one-eighty when it came to work and pleasure.

As a result, Patricia became more efficient and made more money. Patricia's clients enjoyed being with her more since she started having more fun, and the work they did together got done quicker and more pleasurably. Her clients started referring many of their friends and business associates to Patricia, who, they raved, not only could get the work done but made getting it done fun!

The extra bonus for Patricia outside of work was that she found she had more time and energy to date, and enjoyed dating more than ever. This happened because she had replenished her own reserves. Naturally, because Patricia was having more fun, she attracted more men. She looked younger, felt better, and was happier than she had ever been. In the end, Patricia could have been a poster child for the break-time fairy. Does this sound good to you? Well, guess what? You could join her.

My dears, the only way to have more happiness is to cultivate your own garden of wants. Just as a seed needs soil, sun, and water in order to grow, your appetite requires a support system to really spring to life. The best fertilizers you can find for your sprouting desires are fun and pleasure—they are all-natural, and you can never have too much of them, so sprinkle them daily throughout your life. If, as an S.G. in training, you are vigilant about your fun and your pleasure, you will raise your level of sass, friskiness, and confidence, and soon be way more willing to expose what you want, and therefore get it.

I had an interview the other day with the *Sri Lankan Daily Mirror*. The reporter asked me what my message was for the women of Sri Lanka. My message for them is the same as for all women: It's time to serve yourselves first. Most women believe they will get theirs after they serve their jobs, husbands, and families. To be a Sister Goddess, you have to serve yourself first. It is only from that spot that you have the inner clarity, inner surplus, and inner joy to take care of others. Pleasing ourselves is the only answer to our personal happiness and to our happiness as couples or families.

So let's discuss the art of having fun at home. For inspiration, we'll look at the case of S.G. Rachel, a stressed-out, overworked twenty-something mother of three boys, a wife, and a real estate broker. When I first met this gal from Fort Lee, New Jersey, she was running from work to day care, to shop for dinner, to cook dinner, to clean the house—you get the picture. Her husband, a dentist in Fort Lee, was a lovely guy but could not understand how to help his wife more or make her happier. They had not had sex since their eighteen-month-old son was born. Who had time for that, or even for a good conversation with each other? But S.G. Rachel and her husband just kept on keeping on because that's what they thought you were supposed to do. Then Rachel heard about my class and signed up.

After crying through the first three weeks of her Womanly Arts training, S.G. Rachel decided to stop getting sad and mad, and start getting even, by incorporating into her life something we talked a lot about in class—namely, pleasure. Her first move was to hire a baby-sitter—and take a day off from work. She had never done that before. The only time Rachel had ever gotten a baby-sitter was when she and her husband both went to work. Once the baby-sitter arrived, S.G. Rachel drove to the mall. She bought sheets for the baby's crib in order to move the little guy out of her bedroom and into one of his big brothers' rooms. She got a manicure and a pedicure. She bought new lingerie and a sexy new dress. She stopped at the hairdresser and got her hair blown out.

By the time she headed home, S.G. Rachel felt fabulous. At the house, she put the new linens on the baby's bed, took a bath, and kept the baby-sitter on even after she got home. With the night Rachel had planned, neither she nor her husband was going to have any attention to share with their children. By the time her hubby got home Rachel had set out candles, put on music, and slipped into the hot lingerie she had just purchased. Boy, was Rachel's husband surprised! These two had the most romantic hot night they had had since they first met. S. G. Rachel had never bought sexy lingerie before, because her husband said he didn't particularly care for it. What she discovered on this particular evening was that those silky numbers turned her on, and that turned him on.

In some cases men can really get threatened when we start to go our way down the pleasure path. But they have nothing to fear. For as long as there have been men and women, the enormity and intensity of women's desires have been the deciding factor in their lives. In fact, when we women lose our way and stray from our true wants, we usually take a partner or family down with us into the pit of disappointment. We have an incredible power to create, but when we are not pursuing our real desires, the only offspring our creative energy spawns is bitterness and anger. And a lot of it. If, on the other hand, a woman gets what she wants, she usually jumps in and helps others around her feel good, too. S.G. Rachel's husband now, for one, walks around the house saying, "Thank you, Mama Gena," though we have never met.

S.G. Rachel had been enjoying a successful marriage and career. But in reality it just wasn't any fun for her or her husband. When S.G. Rachel decided to prioritize her pleasure, everything became more fun—she enjoyed her family, reignited the flame of passion, and even became more successful at work. S.G. Rachel has continued to be vigilant with pleasure, and now she and her husband are much happier.

Her commitment to pleasuring herself not only got her back together with her husband in a very satisfying way, it had an impact on her work life, too. She had always done well, but she had a sort of laid-back attitude toward her real estate job. She deferred to other people with seniority in her company and generally kept a low profile. Once she had taken control of pleasure in her life, however, her confidence grew, and that affected both her home life and her career. As a student of pleasure, she made it her mission to take on more responsibility and start enjoying her successes.

Around this time of turnaround in her life, S.G. Rachel was at a house waiting for a client when a cute guy in a silver Ferrari sports car drove up, asking her for directions. He mentioned that he was house hunting. She told him how to find the house he was searching for and sent him on his way. As he drove off, she thought to herself, "What am I doing? *He* could be a client!" So she tore off down the street after him, stopping him and giving him her card. The guy liked her, liked her enthusiasm, and she ended up selling a million-dollar home to him. This kind of outrageousness was not at all S.G. Rachel's usual style. It was aggressive, unbelievable even. But she loved the rush of being great, being successful. Focusing on pleasure gave her the room to find her power.

It all started with Rachel pleasuring Rachel. And that, dear Goddesses, is the missing link in all our backgrounds, in all our training. The good news is that our pleasure is always available, it is always at our fingertips, just waiting to be claimed.

When you practice the Womanly Arts you're touching, tasting, smelling, feeling, and experiencing everything life has to offer. You're chomping on life with enthusiasm and learning exactly what pleasures you. Pleasure and fun are the keys not only to your happiness but to the happiness of a relationship, as long as you're committed to putting and keeping yourself first.

As I have said before, at first so many women don't even have a grasp of what it is that pleasures them. You may face a similar situation. Sometimes our fun and pleasure muscles are so undeveloped, they can't even be detected, let alone flexed. The following exercises are designed to strengthen you. See if you can't get your desires into the buff shape they need to be in to deliver to you the happiness, fulfillment, and joy in life that you have been longing for.

Exercise 1: Party with Yourself

Do something for your womanhood, for that lovely female body you have. Your womanhood, your being as a woman, is your responsibility. Mama wants you to explore all of your five senses and the pleasure that they offer.

Have a manicure, a pedicure, or a massage. Make a little party for yourself. Serve your favorite foods and drinks. If you don't know your favorites, this is the time to find out. Buy three kinds of sparkling water and discover your favorite, sample five kinds of chocolate until you have just the right one. Try something you've never tried before—like goat cheese, or olives cured in oil, or chocolate-covered pretzels. Swing out. Put on some great music and dance for no reason. Decorate your body. Put stickers, feathers, ribbons, tattoos, glitter all over your fine self. Dance in celebration of yourself. After all, the party starts with you!

Exercise 2: The Weekly Treat

Schedule one pleasurable thing for yourself a week. If you think there is even the remote chance that you won't stick to this commitment, recruit a girlfriend and create a weekly pleasure check-in call so you can share what pleasure you've enjoyed each week. Outdo each other in the pleasure arena! See what you can do to make a moment that is normally not fun into fun. We all saw that for Patricia, newfound pleasure was a simple as ordering food for what used to be a long, boring meeting. Find out what is fun for you. Maybe it is breaking up your workday with a run through the park or a doughnut run for you and your coworkers! And don't feel as though you have to spend money on these fun things. Sometimes the best and most overlooked pleasures are free: brush your teeth naked and wear high heels, sing along with all your heart to your favorite song, go for a walk with a friend that you love to talk to, meditate before bed, have a make-out session with your favorite kisser! Experiment.

A life without pleasure is about as fulfilling as saltines without the salt (and no dip). It is a life seriously lacking in nutrition. The Goddess requires pleasure to live.

Exercise 3: A Tisket, a Tasket, a Little Pleasure Basket

Create pleasure baskets for the bedroom. Fill them with condoms, lube, sex toys, chocolates, feathers, small towels, and erotica—whatever might make bedtime more fun. You are a sensual Goddess every day, not just when you have company, and your bedroom is command central for sensuality. You want your basket to include fun sensual toys for yourself or for yourself and a partner. You want to have lots of goodies for those yummy nights alone—a bag of Cheetos, your favorite videos. Include some dress-up stuff—a string of pearls, a garter belt, bliss-inducing gear. Make the bedroom your playroom and learn what makes your time there, alone and with others, the most fun.

Exercise 4: Make a Moment That Is Normally Not Fun into Fun for You

Scan your life and look for little moments that you dread or loathe. Think about what you could do to make this unfun activity more fun.

We have had Sister Goddesses wear an evening gown while they do the laundry, have their boyfriends take over the cooking or cleaning, or leave the house forty minutes early so they can walk to work instead of taking the subway. Sister Goddess Katie had a two-hour commute to her office in New Jersey. We had her pack snacks, books on tape, erotica, a cell phone, a sketch pad, a Game Boy, CDs, and a thermos of tea for her trip. Funny—as soon as she began to really enjoy her ride, she got a job offer in the city. Oh, the creative power of fun is not to be underestimated!

Exercise 5: Say Yes to an Offer That You Would Normally Decline

All of us get invitations or offers that we decide we don't have time for, aren't interested in, or that might break up our nice little routine. This week, say *yes* to something that you would not normally say *yes* to. Go out on a limb. Remember, this is research. Just see if you end up enjoying any activities that you don't normally include in your routine. Go to that wine tasting, that girls' night out, that movie screening. You have a better shot at the brass ring when you ride the merry-go-round.

* * *

Fun and pleasure are key ingredients to building a strong foundation for your Sister Goddessliness. Just remember—you can't be fun if you are not having fun. Know that your pleasure is limitless, and that how much fun you have is something you alone control. Why not make a vow to yourself to increase the amount of fun you have over a lifetime? Commit to being an overachiever in the fun department. The nicest thing you can do for another person is to guarantee your own good time. It is the ticket to a gratified, intimate relationship with yourself and others. In the next lesson we will look at how you can introduce deeper vistas of pleasure into your existence, and at their impact on a Goddess's life. Are you ready to discover the jewel in the Goddess crown? If so, follow me, my beauties, for it can be yours!

Lesson 4

The Womanly Art of Sensual Pleasure

Does my sexiness upset you?
Does it come as a surprise
That I dance like I've got diamonds
at the meeting of my thighs?
—Maya Angelou, "Still I Rise"

OK, OK, OK, so how we doin' so far, my S.G's in training? You have come along with Mama to Lesson 4. This could be a parting of the ways with us. Why, you ask? You may begin to banish your dear Mama as I suggest you get to know, and take real ownership of and pleasure in, your velvet underground, your very own sanctum sanctorum.

Remember *Star Trek*—"To boldly go where no man has gone before"? The adventure I propose in this lesson is kind of like that. Only, the place we are boldly going is not a galaxy far, far away, it is a little closer to home. We are charting a course to the place where not every woman has gone before, to the place in which she has the free and fabulous ownership of her sensual self. Let me be perfectly frank. You know how you can know something as well as the back of your hand? That's how well I want you to know your vulva. I want you to know how it looks, in detail, so you could pick yours out of a lineup (should the occasion arise . . .). Actually, I want you to know more about your vulva than you do about the back of your hand. It has way more to offer you.

You know how a dancer knows her body? She knows her flexibility and her strength, and if she learns her instrument really well, her body becomes poetry in motion and sweeps her off her own feet. That's how well a Sister Goddess can learn her sensuality. When you own yourself sensually, everything is open to you. You awaken more feeling in your whole being, experience the joy that is available to you simply because you're a woman. If you are sensually aware, I promise, you are more confident and you enjoy your life more. Some people learn to take exquisite care of their physical exteriors but ignore their sexuality. There is so much taboo. Many of us know more about our teeth or hair than we do about our vulva. Some women think there isn't enough time to have it all. There is. Some women think it is not their responsibility. It is. Some of us were told that our partner would awaken us sensually. That can happen, but only to the extent that you are already awake. Like a dancer, you gotta know how to pirouette on your own to be able to do a pas de deux.

I want to encourage each woman who reads this book to be fluent in every aspect of her physical pleasure. Her sensual body is an eternal wellspring of pleasure. Sensuality is an area where you can make a small investment and get a huge return, or a huge investment and get a life-altering return. The stock market may go up and down, strawberries go in and out of season, fashion go in and out of style, but your sensuality is always there for you—available, and designed for a good time. You don't need a partner to create ecstasy in your body. It doesn't cost anything. It doesn't take a lot of time. By way of shorthand, we are going to call this journey toward knowing and owning yourself sensually "the path to Pussy."

Whaddaya say? Is it a date? Before you slam these pages closed in discomfort or horror, please follow Mama's train of thought for just a moment. Consider that others have put the idea into your mind that "pussy" is a vulgar, uncouth word. I am here to say that, if you accept my definition of it and what it means, "Pussy," with a capital *P,* could be your new favorite word. Really.

"Vulva" identifies the parts. "Pussy," my personal favorite term, identifies more than the parts—it refers to the epicenter of female creativity, physical, emotional, and spiritual. Pussy extends way beyond the crotch. In my world, "Pussy" is a metaphysical term that refers to the essence of female power. Pussy influences how a woman thinks and perceives, how she works and rests, how she relates and communicates. If a woman trusts her Pussy, that means following her instincts and believing in the rightness of her desires.

I have seen women get a whole new perspective on their lives from doing just these things: naming their Pussy, trusting their Pussy, and owning their Pussy. It is both the hardest thing on earth and the simplest, most natural task to allow your body to be your road map to the truth—to trust no value system more than your own elemental physical response. This could be a bold and revolutionary approach to life for you. Imagine feeling so sure of your intuition that you only say *yes* to offers you really want to accept, rather than offers you think you are obliged to accept. Imagine saying *no* with joy and self-approval, rather than guilt or anger. In this light, "Pussy" is a term that can open up an entirely new playing field for you to frolic in.

I realize this concept is not for everyone. If you are not ready for a liberating adventure in the world of Pussy today, you are free to skip this lesson and head for safer ground. Or you can humor Mama and read along, even if you don't actually participate in the exercises. "Pussy" is just a little, much-maligned word, after all. If you'll indulge me, oh indulgent ones, I'll get on with my case. The case for Pussy.

In traditions that go back to the dawn of civilization, the female vulva was revered—as the "magical portal of life, possessed of the power of both physical regeneration and spiritual illumination and transformation" (Riane Eisler, *Sacred Pleasure*). Yup. For thirty to fifty centuries, save the last five thousand years or so, men and women lived in reverence and worship of the Goddess and the power of feminine sensuality. In prehistoric art, vulvas were painted on sacred caves, altars were shaped like the pubic triangle, and religious statuary was designed with especially emphasized vulvas. Humanity perceived feminine power as the animating force of the entire universe. These days we're so unused to this way of thinking, this reverence of the female body's creative portal, that we can't even utter the words that identify it without embarrassment.

During each class, I ask my S.G.'s what "theirs" was called when they were growing up and learning to name their world. Usually, more than half the class say nothing. They say it was just referred to as "down there." But what is not named does not exist. The language we use to identify our body parts (or not) is part of how we learn to respect, accept, and celebrate ourselves.

Of course, I have students whose parents *did* give them names for their body parts. Some are too embarrassed to share the name. Others find the name hilarious. We have had Mrs. Va-Jay-Jay, Knish, Kootchie, Princess Pee Pee, Stinky, Potty, Box, Sassy, Snorker, Hole, Mary, Puppick, Patootie, Jamido, Ya-Ya, and V-Zsa-Zsa. I would laugh, too, if it wasn't so sad. We call a penis "penis." Can you see the roots of a woman's internal chaos when she has nothing but these poor word choices to name the most beautiful and powerful part of her body?

There are always a few S.G.'s I meet who use the word "vagina." At first glance, that term seems like an improvement over the euphemisms, but in fact the term "vagina" refers only to the interior opening of a woman; it does not include any exterior genitalia. It would be the male equivalent of referring to a penis as a scrotum. Not accurate. The word "vagina" actually means "sheath"—you know, the thing a sword goes into. As such, our bodies are considered the supporting cast, rather than the stars of the show. Can you begin to see the spot we are in?

OK, OK, you say, what about "vulva"? This word is certainly more accurate, more to the point. "Vulva" describes the external genitalia of a woman—it includes the labia, inner lips, clitoris, and introitus. When my daughter was two, I taught her to use the word "vulva." I was thrilled and grateful to give her the chance to name her body at her age. I have spent my life searching for my missing parts and feeling more than some degree of embarrassment for my interest. I hope I can save my daughter that long, arduous journey away from and then back to herself.

I want you to take a little tour with me. I want to introduce you to, or reacquaint you with, or simply give an appreciative look at your wondrous Pussy. Grab a hand mirror, get a flashlight, and hit the floor with me now. Close the door and pull those panties off. Part those lips and let's check out the vista. You have a huge range of color possibilities down there, from ruby red to the palest pink, salmon, peach, brown, purple, beige, and blue. The colors of a sunset. There is symmetry, there is asymmetry, just as in nature. I want you to check yourself out with no judgment, only interest and appreciation. Look at the outer lips, the inner lips. See if you can find that little hub of activity, the clitoris, containing eight thousand nerve endings. The clitoris can be tiny or quite large. Usually it is draped modestly in a little fold of skin, called a hood. Behold the pearl. We are starting our journey by looking at what you have, then we will be moving on to seeing how everything works. It is a complete scientific investigation.

It's funny. If I said to you, "I got this Maserati in your garage, and its yours, a gift. And the trunk is full of cash, also yours—and it's always been yours, you just never knew you had it," I know you'd be suspicious at first, but I bet it wouldn't take me ten minutes to talk you into a test drive. You gals have something way more valuable, way more effective in speed and delivery than a car—you have a Pussy—and many of you will want to pass on this lesson, the user's manual to this dream machine of yours, because you will find this topic offensive. Go on with you. Lesson 5 is fun, so's Lesson 6, and so on. You can always come back to this one later.

After all, the idea of a woman knowing and pleasuring herself has not been in vogue for thousands of years. Taking full control of your body and your pleasure is no small shakes. It's a helluva gear shift, gals. But don't judge yourself if you're hesitant to jump in for the ride of your life. We're taught to sit back and let someone else drive. The truth is, when you think someone outside you controls your pleasure, you feel out of control. At nineteen I wasn't sure if I was having sex with my boyfriend because I wanted to or because it was expected of me. I was curious, but I wasn't sure what were the signals to follow; all my close girlfriends were doing it, so I did, too. A lot of women have shared stories of similar experiences with me. If you think your boyfriend or girlfriend or gynecologist or mother knows more about your sexual nature or genitals than you do, you are in big, big trouble. You can't own what you think someone else possesses. Unless you own your sensuality, you will only be dependent or needy or desperate in your couplings. True partnership comes only after true ownership.

We keep hoping the next generation of women will have it easier and better than us. And they do. We could make it even easier and better for the women maturing today by deciding to take ownership of our sensuality now. Of the hundreds upon hundreds of S.G.'s who have crossed my threshold, not one has ever been ignorant of how to pleasure a penis (or confessed to such ignorance, anyway). But almost all of them have been ignorant when it came to pleasuring themselves, and close to despairing over how to teach their partners to pleasure them. I am not saying these women are necessarily inorgasmic—they simply have not investigated their own pleasure with the same sense of obligation, righteousness, and freedom that they have investigated a man's pleasure.

This not only puts women at a disadvantage but prevents men from ever learning what a woman truly is. If a woman will not learn and live what a woman is, how can her male counterpart come to fully understand her? I want you to learn about Pussy—the care, the feeding, and the pleasuring thereof. Go at your pace. You are your own best guide. And before you bail out of this lesson on me, if you are still with me, let me share one observation that I've noticed since starting my School of Womanly Arts. I have actually found in the last three years of my work, with hundreds of S.G.s, that the ones who resist this information the most at the beginning actually end up getting the most out of it at the end.

So let's move our research from the visual inventory to the manual operation. I am not interested in masturbation. I am interested in self-pleasuring. The word "masturbation" has a lot of baggage and a goal orientation about it that will actually hinder our progress. I want you to start with a clean slate with me. First of all, create a clean, private sanctuary for you to do your self-pleasuring. Prepare yourself. Take a bath, put on a nightie or robe. Moisturize your velvety skin, dab yourself with perfume if that pleases you. Light a candle, put on some lovely music. Avoid alcohol, because alcohol is a sensation depressant, and we want all your senses in top working order. You can begin with your hand mirror to check out your Pussy, because I want you to see it before, during, and after you stroke yourself. Your Pussy will change. The clit will engorge, the lips will darken as they fill with blood during arousal, and the whole area will get puffier and fuller and more voluptuous looking. When you begin to touch yourself, I want you to use your hand as if it was a pleasure-seeking device. Most of us try to deliver pleasure without touch. That is working too hard. I want you to take pleasure with your hand. Selfish hand. Let it run across your pubic hair as if it were touching a kitten's fur. Let it swirl and twirl. Gently spread your lips and let those fingers caress the delicate skin of your lips. Try it without lubricant, and then try it with lubricant. (I am a lube fan.) Take those fingers on a tour of your inner lips, your introitus, and your clitoris. Touch your clitoris through the hood, and then pull the hood back and touch the surface directly. I really recommend lube at this point; the genital tissue is very delicate, and very resilient. I want you to try every kind of pressure you can imagine—

from the lightest feather to the heaviest pinch. See what you like, and where you like it. You can do this research for just five minutes, or much longer. You decide. And don't forget to get that hand mirror and watch how your Pussy changes as it is pleasured. And when you touch yourself, remember that your goal is simply to create pleasurable sensation for as long as possible.

The only function of the clitoris is pleasure. It is not at all involved in reproduction. After all, women can become pregnant without orgasms. In fact, the majority of women have intercourse without orgasm because the penis usually doesn't contact the clitoris during intercourse, and as most of us know, male orgasm usually has no impact on the clitoris either.

Compared to the clitoris, the penis is a multitool. Take a look—the penis ejaculates, it urinates, and it experiences only four thousand nerve endings' worth of pleasure, half the amount of the clitoris. The fact that the clitoris is for and about pleasure and only pleasure is the reason why it has been excluded, until very recently, from medical anatomy books. Each woman's clitoris, as different as it is from all the others out there, does have a lot in common with its sister clits. For example, it does not get diseased. It does not atrophy. No matter what its size and shape, each glorious clitoris has the ability to have unlimited orgasms, once it is properly fired up and instructed. Understand and love the clitoris and you will understand and love woman.

The clitoris and her special purpose—pleasure—is a great metaphor for the Sister Goddess. This organ of pleasure that we women have wants what every woman wants—attention, attention, attention. The clit wants to be touched exactly the way it likes it best, which usually involves about half the pressure that most men use. Think about it—most men learn the art of sexual gratification with their own bodies as a reference (it's only natural), but they have only half the nerve endings in their sexual pleasure area that we women have in ours.

We have learned pleasure from male partners, too, and many of us have been limited by what we experience with them. Whereas a man can have a few brief moments of orgasmic bliss, a woman can have hours upon hours of orgasm. He is a revolver, she is a semiautomatic. But even though women are capable of an extended period of sexual pleasure, it doesn't mean that they are achieving it. In fact, most women have yet to experience their true sexual potential.

Because women learn to compromise even before they learn to come, few women have felt their own true sexual pleasure erupt, like Mount Saint Helens, or crash wave after wave, like the ocean. When a woman comes like a man—all at once, like a sneeze—she limits the range of feeling possible for her by virtue of her unique physiology. Men's sexuality is goal driven rather than pleasure driven. Women need to get in touch with the undulating, ever expanding, pulsating world of female orgasm, and to come as only a woman can—an experience not to be missed! What most women need is the owner's manual for their very own sexual equipment.

The instruction manual for a clit reads: "Educate yourself about me. Observe, listen, explore, appreciate, investigate. If you love what I, the clitoris, am feeling, I will feel more, and more, and more." When women follow these simple rules, they quickly learn that the clit won't turn on when it is upset, angry, or scared. It won't be forced, or respond to abuse. If you try to rush the clit, it does not cooperate. If you disapprove of the amount this pleasure center is feeling, it feels less. So, what are the optimal working conditions for the clitoris? Optimal is when the woman is operating at full throttle—engorged, infused with life and enthusiasm—when she is capable of total, full-on communication, able to say "Stop it" and "More!" and everything in between without hesitation.

Like flying a kite or playing an instrument, just do it as long as it is fun. Then stop. And do it again, sometime, soon. I recommend a rather steady diet of self-pleasuring. Women look beautiful when they begin to spend their energy in pleasurable ways. It is a great tension reducer and mood enhancer. And if you continue to pay attention to your ever-changing body, you will find wonderful sensations that you can then teach to a partner.

* * *

Let me tell you an inspirational tale about one of the hardest nuts that ever crossed Mama's path. She arrived as Mattie Diamond, financial analyst, Wall Street. But Mama could see there was a wild woman buried inside this buttoned-down, buttoned-up Diva. Mattie's heroine is Madonna, and once in a while she would have a divalike tantrum and thus become S.G. Madonna, her alter ego. Actually, S.G. Madonna is an adorable cross between a kooky Diane Keaton character and Linda Blair, just before the exorcism. She lives to gossip and thus became the gossip columnist of the Sister Goddess network. She has a column that she posts monthly on our Web site. In order to live fully in her new role as celebrity columnist, she renamed herself Sister Goddess Prada Madonna, or Sister Goddess PMS for short. (This was a great combination of Mattie's two loves—shopping and show business.)

Anyway, back to the story. Sometimes there are Sister Goddesses who take the course and enjoy it but who never really do their homework. The class is entertaining enough, even if you just sit in the bleachers and watch the other women become Goddesses. Well, S.G. Mattie spent her first few of Mama Gena's classes in the bleachers. S.G. Mattie was willing to buy new makeup but unwilling to pleasure her Pussy. She skipped that part. S.G. Mattie could not intellectually understand why masturbation and paying attention to pleasing herself sensually was important. It simply was not logical to her. After all, S.G. Mattie had been an analyst on Wall Street for years. If she was going to move on something, it *had* to be logical. So for years S.G. Mattie hung around watching other S.G.'s rocket into space while she lingered, somewhat bitterly, on earth, recording their every fantastic move.

One day, my Goddesses and I came up with the concept of "slave drivers." There were S.G.'s who were doing great—leaping and bounding into their dreams—and they agreed to coach the slugs. S.G. Mattie, being the slowest of the slow, got S.G. Justine, who was moving pretty damn fast. Justine called Mattie every single day. Justine would inquire, cajole, and threaten her pupil, and got S.G. Mattie to actually touch her own Pussy for the first time. Ever.

During the first week of Justine's mentoring, Mattie masturbated three times and, miraculously, received three job offers and a date. The second week S.G. Mattie upped her self-pleasuring to four times, and the date invited her to Paris for the weekend. Well, S.G. was on a roll and really feeling great about it.

The amazing thing is that I just ran into S.G. Mattie as I was writing this chapter. She tells me that she is now dating a guy who she has known for ten years, who lives in her building, and who is Italian and sexy, and she is mad for him! S.G. Mattie also shared with me that she just had the best blind date of her life, last week. It lasted seven hours! And yes, my new rising star, Mattie, is still going out with the guy who invited her to Paris. She told me that she has kept up with her self-pleasuring—in fact she masturbated three times that week. She still maintains masturbation does not make logical sense to her. But the boost to her overall joy is undeniable. The sensual path she has started upon has even improved this S.G.'s gossip column. Mattie's writing is even funnier because she can tease people lovingly, now that she is finding happiness for herself.

That's what S.G. Emily, an actress, is now doing. But when she first attended my classes, Emily was most definitely not pleasuring herself. She was also having lots of auditions, but coming up short when it came to landing the roles she wanted. Emily came from a very conservative Waspy Mayflower background. She never looked at her Pussy or touched it—she experienced her crotch only when a boyfriend touched her. S.G. Emily decided to really investigate her pleasure—as a business tool. She thought it might help her career if she owned her sensuality.

So, Emily took on pleasuring herself every day. Then, guess what happened. She got another audition—this time the director loved her so much that he was thinking of rewriting the script so Emily could play the part (it was written for a woman ten years older than she was). In the end, he could not do that. The really interesting thing about this whole episode was S.G. Emily's response—instead of being depressed again after not making the cut, she was elated! This Sister Goddess was so proud that she had gotten that far in the audition process and that the director had loved her so much.

Throughout this experience, Emily noticed her moods and her ability to deal with the ups and downs of life had changed completely. This budding Sister Goddess found she could now find the positive in any situation much more quickly than she ever could before.

Emily's whole outlook was much happier, much more confident. She had taken control of her life simply by taking control of the pleasure in it, and taking the responsibility of practicing self-gratification.

The very next thing that happened to our gal S.G. Emily was she had a successful audition that led to a starring role in a feature film. Her big break! S.G. Emily knows she brought her own big break into being by taking control of her pleasure.

The moral of these stories of ecstasy lost and ecstasy found is that noticing is all. When we pretend mediocre life is sufficient, we give up our shot at ecstasy. I know it can sometimes seem easier to do the conventional thing and compromise yourself instead of taking on the responsibility of self-gratification. Most of us have been in that place. But when you notice and trust your desires, they will set you on the right path. And the journey toward knowing yourself is not complete until you know and own your sensuality. This is the truth of the matter, as difficult as it may be to admit and sign up for. But don't beat yourself up for resisting your own pleasure or feeling inadequate to reclaim it. You don't get much support on this front at all—but you can relax a bit now because yo' mama is here to help!

How truly solo we often are on the road of self-gratification. That's downright unhinged. Our culture encourages us to know how to do so many things: read, write, add, subtract, operate a computer, manage a career, raise children. We have cooking schools, dog obedience schools, wine tasting schools; pottery, ballet, and music schools; and gyms with personal trainers. We are informaholics. You wouldn't even think of giving your sixteen-year-old kid keys to the family car until he or she took driver's ed. We want plumbers to have licenses, the people who teach our schools to have degrees. The only area in which we actually encourage and promote ignorance is sensuality and pleasure.

My mama taught me about menstruation but she sure never mentioned that we both had a clitoris. She told me to beware of boys and what they might want from me—but she never taught me how to really enjoy kissing one. I know my mama was way ahead of her mama, giving me information. I got very little, but she got even less.

Women are taught to have a lot of shame about their sensuality. Sensuality and pleasure are areas that most women don't talk about, don't feel comfortable with. What if our greatest shame were actually our greatest source of pride and joy? Before you deny your sensuous side, or feel too uncomfortable to explore it, or think you can have the upper hand without getting in touch with it, think again about what I said about that free Maserati. Why don't you at least consider taking your sensual self for a test drive? The keys are in your hands. Is it worth it to you to experiment? I invite you to take the plunge!

Mama's got some exercises for you to raise your level of self-adoration, gratitude, and worship of the wonder of your own body. You cannot 'help' someone love themselves until you, your sexy-assed self, take the step. As Gandhi said, "*Be* the change in the world you wish to see." As I see it, the seat of a woman's power is her relationship to her own erotic nature. From a mass media saturated with images of what our bodies should look like to our culture's extremely ambivalent attitudes toward sexuality, it is not easy for women to accept, embrace, and enjoy their bodies. Yet the extent to which we own our sensuality is the extent to which we own our lives. When we know and love ourselves completely and intimately, physically, emotionally, spiritually, sensually, we have a competitive advantage. We have more control. When you are trained to ignore yourself, you will ignore details that are crucial. Explore these exercises and ignore yourself no more!

Exercise 1: The Artist's Way

Grab some Play-Doh, glitter glue, paint, crayons, markers, and pencils and take yourself back to kindergarten arts and crafts. Only, this time, the subject matter is your vulva. Paint, shape, draw, sketch your vulva. You can be symbolic—drawing it like a flower or a flame—or specific, including all the shapely parts. (Don't forget the clitoris and it won't forget you!) For extra credit, hang your work of art on a wall. It is quite a conversation piece! This assignment will have you get in touch with and celebrate your power source.

Exercise 2: Spring Cleaning

Remember this exercise from Lesson 2? Bring it back. This time, do the exercise exactly the same way, but your topic is "sensuality." So your sentence would read, "What do I have on 'sensuality'?" Do it for twenty minutes, alone, with a friend, or with a group of friends.

Exercise 3: Owner's Manual

Buy a copy of the book *Extended Massive Orgasm* by Drs. Vera and Steve Bodansky. They take you through a thorough, scientific, informational journey about pleasure. You will learn to name each part of your vulva, what it can do for you, and how to deliver the best possible self-pleasure and partnered pleasure. This is a must read for the serious sensual citizen!

Exercise 4: Mirror, Mirror

Now, my dear Sister Goddesses in training, I have saved the best for last. The most important step in becoming a Sister Goddess is owning your crotch.

But before you begin your exploration, you will want to pay exquisite attention to your health. You won't enjoy anything if you have unaddressed concerns about your well-being. So make that long-overdue appointment with the gynecologist. Be responsible and do what it takes to feel as fabulous as you humanly can. When a woman is separated from the rightness of her vulva, her essential nature, she loses the key to knowing, feeling, and trusting her desires.

So how do you take ownership of this region, this terrain, this magnificent vista that we barely can see? How do you tell what true appetite is? A hand mirror's worth at a time, my dear. Lie in a well-lit area with a hand mirror and spread your legs. The following are some potential responses as you pursue your self-investigation:

- You're revolted—a common response. How many of us look "down there" regularly? The colors may shock you. The hair growth may surprise you. If you are revolted, you are way far from being a Sister Goddess. Sister Goddesses ADORE and WORSHIP their crotches. They believe Courbet was right when he titled his painting, *L'Origine du monde*. Whaddaya know? Take a scientific approach. Observe. Don't judge. Sit in your Pussy's presence and watch and feel. Make no strong judgments or hasty moves. She will grow on you.

- You are indifferent. No problem. You are just numb to your own greatness, your own power. Probably because your potential is so huge. One woman, who now works with Mama, couldn't even feel anything in her crotch when she touched herself. She found the whole thing kind of ugly. She would have dropped out of the class completely if she had not seen other women getting such remarkable results from falling in love with themselves. Yo' mama had her observe Pussies in paintings, in flowers. Her approval grew. It grew to the point where she broke up with the guy who was having sex with her purely for his gratification and she started to date a guy who actually paid attention to her pleasure.

- You like it. Wow, you are way, way down the Sister Goddess trail! All there is to do now is like it more. Sister Goddess Diane, an agent for designer clothing companies, came to class as a regular self-pleasuring enthusiast, really appreciating herself. As she allowed herself to fall more in love with her crotch, she found she was more in tune with herself. As this process unfolded, as she became aware of her true desires, she saw that there was a connection between her approval of herself and her outer experiences. Her confidence radiated. She went from selling about $5,000 per month to $15,000 to $20,000. She wanted to meet a designer from another company, and within a week he called her and arranged a trip for her to go to Europe and sell clothing for him. Coincidence? Maybe. Mama calls it the power of desire or the power of

Pussy or simply the power of "P." The more you own and appreciate your Pussy, the more it delivers for you.

Exercise 5: Between the Covers

Explore the ideas of other brave, pleasure-seeking S.G.'s by reading such works as

The Vagina Monologues, by Eve Ensler, a fun, moving experience of sisterhood through vaginas. You can read it in an hour and it will make you even happier about your crotch.

Women's Bodies, Women's Wisdom, by Christiane Northrup, the Bible for women. If you want to know the delicious details of how we function, the genius of our bodies, and what to do when something breaks down—this book is for you.

Woman: An Intimate Geography, by Natalie Angier, a book that will have you reveling in the glory, the power, and the beauty of what a woman is. You will feel moved and elated at the elegant prose.

Sacred Pleasure, by Riane Eisler, describes the historical impact of women, specifically the early Goddess religions and their roots in pleasure and partnership versus our pain-oriented culture of today. Read it and your eyes will open to possibilities you may never have considered before!

Your access to Pussy is your access to your own life force, your freedom as a woman and as a human being. Taking control of yourself for your ultimate pleasure is the new-millennium equivalent to unbinding your feet; it creates a power in you that you may never have enjoyed before. What to do with all this new unbridled power? How about a new game . . . the art of flirtation? To find out how to play, turn to the next lesson. I promise that you'll be enchanted with this empowering form of entertainment!

Lesson 5

The Womanly Art of Flirtation

Darling, the legs aren't so beautiful, I just know what to do with them.

—Marlene Dietrich

The lesson for today is about Flirtation. A woman is in her highest, most glorious state when she flirts. Women are born to flirt, destined to flirt. Flirting is in a woman's DNA. And she will flirt with anyone when she feels like it—her child, her poodle, her neighbor, her girlfriends, her men. My baby girl began flirting when she first became aware of people. No one, except perhaps her mama, has Papa so wrapped around her little finger as my little girl does.

Flirtation is also an art. Flirtation lightens the spirit. It is the quickest way out of a jam—you can melt arguments, evaporate traffic tickets, win a spot at a crowded restaurant. Flirtation eases communication. It makes whatever you wish come to you more smoothly.

Flirtation is a woman's access to the life force. It is a simple, fun way to be at your most powerful, to have your way with people, to achieve the most fulfilling, enjoyable, spontaneous life possible. A woman who flirts can turn any *no* into a *yes.* A woman in the act of flirtation can beguile the entire world with her enthusiasm. She is in a state of her highest glory. She looks beautiful, she is always having fun, she feels powerful. She senses what is right for herself and others, she trusts her instincts. She needs no man, no one, and she can enjoy everyone around her. She demands the best from herself and others, knowing that gratification is not only possible, it is her birthright. Are you not humble before your own talents? It's not just Helen of Troy who could launch a thousand ships. Baby, it's you!

Flirting is a whole-body experience. A woman flirts from the tips of her toes to the top of her head, and everywhere in between. She feels good, and everyone around her does, too. Think Mae West, think Julia Roberts's smile. Each woman flirts in her own, inimitable way. She shows her approval of herself and others in a way that suits her. Some women tilt the head; some have more direct, eye-to-eye contact; some glance away—none of the *how* matters. You will locate your own wonderful style. It is a matter of loving yourself, enjoying the world around you, and picking someone and letting them have it, full blast. You can't flirt from the neck up. If you do fake it, you look a bit like the queen greeting her subjects. Pay attention to the person you are talking to, and take the attention off yourself. If you pay attention to the other person, you can mesmerize them. This is integral to the fulfillment of your desires. If you can see where someone is at, you can bring them into your vision.

When I begin a new Goddess class, opening night, no one is feeling flirtatious, except for my own fine self and my bevy of assistants. The first-nighters are scared, doubtful, worried that they've lost their minds by signing up for such a class. Doubt is a big enemy of flirtation.

And most women, I've found, live more or less constantly in a state of doubt.

But the truth is, women are the source in the flirtation department. No guy ever gets a piece of ass without a woman beckoning him, inviting him toward her on some level. (I am deliberately excluding rape here. Rape is a violent act, not a sensual encounter.) We women have all the cards. We control the game. We are the hunters, not the hunted, even when we make it look the other way round.

You know how it goes. You see a cute guy at a bar. You think, "Hmm . . . looks good." He feels you thinking that thought—wanting something from him. Next thing you know, he's over to you in a flash. "Can I buy you a drink?" he asks. And you let him think it was his idea. In the man/woman game, women are the igniters, guys the responders. We ladies have the ability to call—to invite through our desires. Flirtation creates a physical response.

Now, you may be saying to yourself, "How can this be? This sounds a bit too simple, too good to be true." Well, my doubting beauties, all you have to do is look to man's best friend to see the truth of it. That's right, dogs can teach us more about this new trick. You have all seen the transformation of Old Blue, the gray-muzzled, fifteen-year-old dog sleeping on the porch day in, day out—until Princess, the poodle next door, goes into heat. Then Old Blue suddenly leaps into action, tail wagging. He's off to the races, barking, running, leaping, all in the name of Princess. His puzzled owners haven't seen him run around like this in years. When Princess is out of heat, Blue returns to snoring on the porch. Notice that Old Blue doesn't have to consummate his desire for Princess in order to get a surge of energy—he just has to be in the vicinity when she is feeling her most female, creative, natural self.

Human beings are not all that different. Humans can create excitement just by thinking about what excites them. No other mammals can do that. You know how it works: when you are going out on a date, you spend hours primping and making yourself gorgeous, and by the time you get to the restaurant with your new date, you can barely eat, you are so excited. As you begin to put the pedal to the metal, you will notice that you can tap into the power of flirtation at any time. And believe me, when you do, people will notice. They, too, will be affected by your magnetism.

Unfortunately, some women find their powers of attraction unsettling, even unwanted. Women tend to keep the lid on their magnetism, for very good reasons. First, there's the obligation thing: "If he finds me attractive, then he'll ask me out, and even if I don't want to, I should say *yes* so I don't offend him." Or, "What if no one else asks me? At least I have him." Yikes! Not much fun. Or then there's, "If I turn him on, maybe I have to sleep with him." Double yikes! Or then there's, "If he gets turned on and his behavior becomes inappropriate, maybe it's my fault." Triple yikes. We are raised to think that our personal charms are for the use of men and not for our own pleasure and entertainment. We have grown up being told that the sexy part of ourselves is bad or wrong, not the essence of our nature. And when we internalize that message, and get bound up in too much work, too much pressure, stress, or obligation, our flirting facility shuts down. Luckily you can rewire your circuitry so that your energy is focused on your entertainment, your fun, and your fulfillment. You can't fake fun, that's the thing. When you create your life to include it, it shows, because you glow.

One of my former S.G.'s—an advertising executive, S.G. Clarissa—had completely banished flirtation from her life. She was militant in her conviction that flirtation did not and would not exist for her. Clarissa felt she needed to be serious in order to control her job and rise in her career. Of course, this actually made her totally out of control. She was seeing a therapist, taking Prozac; the only way Clarissa could relax was to have a drink and avoid dating altogether. I know that S.G. Clarissa is just one of many women who have chosen to suppress much of who they are. But I am here to tell you that killing your relationship to flirtation is not only stifling, it is downright harmful. It would be the equivalent of clipping a bird's wing and asking it to fly, never mind asking it to be happy.

How can you tell how much flirtation you are letting loose in your life now? Well, how happy are you, on a scale of one to ten? If you are depressed, if you are uncertain that you could make every head in the restaurant turn to look at you as you make your entrance, if you don't feel confident you could flirt your way out of a traffic ticket or your way into a crowded nightclub, then you are accepting less than you deserve as a woman. No matter what you look like, or how young or old you are, simply by virtue of being born a woman you possess all the equipment you need to have your way in every aspect of your life. For true happiness, a woman wants to have her way everywhere—from the boardroom to the bedroom.

Change is just a mind-set away for each one of us, my beauties. For you have the power to control the attention.

The problem is, we don't usually touch our control panel unless there's a human object of desire around. Well, we could exercise those dials a lot more. We all would benefit from cranking them up or down, getting to know their settings very well, and using them on a daily basis, regardless of whether a new partner is one foot away or one hundred miles from us.

Flirtation is something that you, as a woman, are in control of and that you can use whenever, wherever you are. When you go to a restaurant with a bunch of friends, you have the power to make every head in that restaurant turn to look at you as you make your entrance. Your impact on that room has no relationship to pretty. It has no relationship to age. It has to do only with how much you are approving of yourself and, consequently, approving of the other people in your universe. If you love your sensual self you can make others notice its gorgeousness as well. Flirtation is nothing more or less than enthusiastic self-love and experiencing it in every fiber of your being, and allowing that love to overflow to others.

It's an energy you radiate, not unlike a lightbulb on a dimmer switch. When you find yourself walking a deserted stretch of street, or taking the bus late at night, for instance, you turn your dial way, way down so that you become almost invisible. You lower your enthusiasm level and pull your focus inward.

I once went backstage to see a friend who was starring in a one-woman show. Bette Midler and her husband were also backstage, as well as other admirers. Bette had her light switch off. No one saw her. She was invisible. The second our friend the star appeared, she suddenly came to life, and became the dazzling, adorable Bette. Suddenly flashbulbs went a-poppin' as people recognized her. After greeting our friend she became invisible again, and left. You all have that level of control over your personal magnetism. Keep practicing, be deliberate.

The fact is that flirtation is all about you having more fun. Your goal is to amuse yourself, which naturally lightens the atmosphere for everyone. Everyone benefits from a good flirt. The gift of flirting leaves the giver refreshed and the receiver enhanced.

Evelyn, a fifty-something, semidivorced S.G. from Long Island, had also totally forgotten about her flirting ability. It was buried under decades of festering frustration. S.G. Evelyn had been pissed at her husband for as long as she could remember. Like doubt, anger is another enemy of flirtation, and the cost of this prolonged anger was primarily hers to bear. Evelyn had forgotten herself, the best parts of herself—you know, the cute, adorable, vital, powerful, juicy parts of herself. When I met her, S.G. Evelyn looked pale and asexual. She told me, when I asked her, that her underwear drawer was full of worn-out Carter's. Her clothes were functional and buttoned up. There was no *joie* in her *vivre.* But S.G. Evelyn put Mama Gena's techniques to work and changed her whole world from drab to sparkling. From a drag to great fun! One of the exercises that turned S.G. Evelyn's world around was Bitte et Chat.

Yes, to practice the art of flirtation, we have an assignment in class—affectionately called "Bitte et Chat." The S.G.'s are asked to walk into any store, any office, any parking lot, and—just for the fun of it—let themselves flirt. You all know how to do this thing. It's very simple. You just look at your deli guy and think pleasant, delicious thoughts about your body, or maybe even his body. You can direct your thoughts in any way you want—any way that makes you feel good. Your friends at the deli counter won't know what exactly you are up to, they will just know they are magnetically drawn to you. They will enjoy your attention and have the feeling that you are noticing what is best about them. Like magic, they will leap to get you what you want, jump over themselves, actually.

It was not long after employing this game of Bitte et Chat that S.G. Evelyn began to come to life. She soon had her deli guy well trained. Now, as she walks in the door, he's handing her her coffee exactly the way she likes it, no matter what kind of line is in front of her. In fact, Evelyn so enjoyed the enthusiasm of his response, she secretly took her new techniques into work with her. She gave Tony, the super, a big smiling hello as she created good feelings in her crotch. He was touched to the quick. Evelyn's warmth toward Tony continued as she found herself enjoying it. The next week, in fact, he appeared at work with a toupee, looking rather dashing and rakish. S.G. Evelyn appreciated his new look. The next day, he had a box of doughnuts, and he offered first pick to Evelyn. Coincidence? Maybe. But S.G. Evelyn is enjoying the hell out of all her knights in shining armor. And they are enjoying it, too. She loves this newfound power. Evelyn doesn't owe Tony the super a date, nor does he expect one. Or the deli guy or even her car dealer, who does her bidding. It is simply a pleasure to take care of a Goddess as she enjoys being a Goddess. All of these men are basking in this gal's fresh sparkle. S.G. Evelyn isn't the only one enjoying Tony's toupee. Tony enjoys it and so do Tony's wife and kids.

S.G. Eve had just broken up with her boyfriend when she took her first Mama Gena course. In fact, her best friend, Annie, dragged her to the class. Absorbed in her great misery, she did not feel at all in the mood to flirt when she got the Bitte et Chat assignment. In fact, the homework made her want to crawl into a hole. S.G. Annie suggested they get together that night, get dressed up, and go to a party. S.G. Eve whined but cooperated. They met at Annie's and had a hilarious time choosing outfits and doing makeup. They decided that all they would do at the party was their homework—which was simply to practice flirting. This was not about dating, not about finding a boyfriend, not about making new friends. This was about using their own ability to enjoy themselves, delight in themselves, and turn themselves on for their own pleasure. No other agenda. It was downright liberating.

They got to the party, feeling fantastic. They were already having so much fun. Eve and Annie found themselves to be the most enchanting, incredible women at the party. It seemed everyone wanted to talk to them. S.G. Annie was stunned as she watched S.G. Eve get this tall Saudi man in a caftan to bring her a glass of wine, while she was flirting with his best friend. When Eve went to find Annie, she was sitting on a leather wing-back chair while one guy held her drink and the other fed her hors d'oeuvres. Perhaps the highlight of the evening, for S.G. Eve, was that, after she gave the Saudi her phone number, this cute French guy escorted her to her car, asked for her number, and she ended up making out with him in the parking lot. Who was that guy she was all broken up about earlier that day?? What was his name???

Flirtation is so much a part of what a woman is, who a woman is, that its power can surpass a woman's own doubts about herself if she gives in to it. S.G. Bess was sixty-five years old in her first M.G. course. She said she did not think she ever flirted—in her entire life. Being a pragmatic woman, she decided "What the hell, I'll give it a try!!" and proceeded to put on a little lipstick and cock her beret to one side as she took her poodle, Fluffy, for a walk that night. She started the experiment of smiling. Smiling at everyone. She winked at the guy at the newspaper stand, stopped and chatted with the guy waiters at her favorite café, and generally had herself a most magnificent stroll about town. On her way back Fluffy got into the act. She must have felt some of Bess's new-found sassiness because when a fellow dog walker reached down to pat Fluffy, she lunged for him and jumped on his lap. S.G. Bess was shocked, then delighted. The guy was twenty years younger than she, also a dog owner, also single. They have been having a wonderful e-mail flirtation about their frisky dogs ever since Fluffy made their introduction!

The fact is, flirting also empowers you. A woman in touch with this fantastic force is deeply alive. She doesn't wait for a man to be around to tap into her power, she does not wait to unleash it behind the bedroom door. No, she will trot that power out anytime, anywhere it can help, entertain, amuse, or empower her. Most women were taught to flirt when they want something from someone. But flirting is not currency. It is an activity that is done for the sheer pleasure of it, not necessarily with any goal in mind. Flirtation with a goal in mind isn't flirtation, it's work. Will wonderful things happen to you if you flirt? Absolutely. Will you get many great offers? Absolutely. But that is not the reason to flirt. It is done for the sheer pleasure of it all.

What you need to know is that the fun is in you, darlings. You can bring it out with . . . practice, practice, practice! In the spirit of the task that is before you, Mama has created some inspirational exercises to get you all hot and bothered with your fine self.

Exercise 1: Setting Your Turn-on Dial

Do a little Bitte et Chat. Go out there in the world, pick a totally safe circumstance like the man in the glass booth at the subway station, and when you ask for directions, think of your own delicious body. Notice how it makes you feel. Notice how he responds. When you walk into a restaurant, ask your boss for a raise, call the phone company—think pleasurable thoughts about your crotch. Notice your response and the response of your "victim." Don't just practice turning your dial way up; practice turning it way down, like when you have to travel alone at night.

Exercise 2: Flirting Tips from the Pros

Rent *I'm No Angel* with Mae West. Watch how she uses her feminine appeal (despite her size, her age) to get the guy she wants! What do you suppose she's thinking about when she's flirting with all these men? Yes, darlings, they had Bitte et Chat in the 1930s. Rent *Basic Instinct* and watch Sharon Stone. Then go out and practice. Try turning on the guy behind the deli counter at the supermarket. Notice how this makes you feel (not him, you!). Use your basic instincts.

Exercise 3: Flirting with Yourself

Get in touch with what personally turns you on. What is your favorite taste sensation? Have your favorite food this week. If it's practical, put a favorite taste (like chocolate or a lollipop) in your pleasure basket. Do a Spring Cleaning on "flirting" to further get in touch with your thoughts and feelings about the turn-on. Out with the old, in with the new.

* * *

Most women do not take control of this particular womanly art. A Sister Goddess can start practicing and run with it! Now that you're warmed up in the flirtation department, it is time to take control of your body image. You can use flirtation as a magic wand to make yourself beautiful. Who wouldn't like to be even more beautiful than she is right now? Keep reading and find out how.

Lesson 6:

The Womanly Art of Owning Your Beauty

> There is a fountain of youth: It is your mind, your talents, the creativity you bring to your life and the lives of the people you love. When you learn to tap this source, you will truly have defeated age.
>
> —Sophia Loren

Ownership is the key to beauty. You gotta dig on down and own yours to have yours. Every Sister Goddess—no matter how beautiful the world tells her she is—has to know and accept herself if she is to get hold of her own special brand of beauty, if she is to truly own it. Loving ourselves releases our life force and expands our beauty.

Our innate beauty is nothing without enthusiasm backing it up. That's why some women who have great physical attributes do not strike us as particularly attractive, and why some women who have no objective reason to enchant come across as absolutely, drop-dead gorgeous. Most of us fall somewhere in between, but all of us can swing from beauty to ugliness, depending on our mood. I was always amazed, for instance, at how Judy Garland's appearance could change from one photo to the next. I'm not talking about bad- and good-hair days here. Sometimes Judy looked movie-idol gorgeous, and other times—sometimes in a photo shot just days after one that was stunning—she was almost shockingly ugly. Her features were the same, so what changed? I think on those days when Judy was loving Judy, she looked fabulous, and on days when Judy didn't love Judy, she could look like absolute hell.

Beauty isn't as simple to achieve as a plastic surgeon, an orthodontist, a personal trainer, a modeling agency, or today's women's magazines might have you think. It isn't all in the measurements, my lovelies. Look at poor Jennifer Grey—she was so cute with her hook nose in *Dirty Dancing*. The world fell in love with her unique beauty. Too bad she didn't see it. Now, after her nose job, she may have come closer to conventional beauty, but in changing her particular combination of features, she seems to have diminished her beauty.

Beauty's elusive trick, her secret, is that she requires great internal discipline to exist. Loving all of the features we have—the perfect, the quirky, the downright ugly—is one decision that creates her. Setting the stage for beauty, creating the atmosphere, being deliberate about every aspect of her care and feeding all contribute to beauty's ongoing existence. Pleasure in life, satisfaction with ourselves, frequent orgasms, and a rich sensual life add to her glow. We are all capable of radiating our own individual beauty into the world, we all have access to the glow of gorgeousness. The question becomes, how *interested* are we in being beautiful? Are we interested enough to accept ourselves completely in order to be a knockout? Consider this seriously, my beauties, for complete ownership of ourselves and all our gifts is the price that beauty exacts.

The issue of ownership of our beautiful selves often comes up in my early Goddess classes. I ask my Goddesses to share their stories of coming to terms with their individual beauty. S.G. Lane is a model who had a great story of ownership to tell her Sister Goddesses in training one evening. She told us that she wanted to be a model from the time she was a girl. Dressing up her Barbie dolls was an inspiration to her. When she became a teenager, Lane would hang out in New York City and try to meet and mingle with the whole fashion crowd. She submitted her photos to many modeling agencies, but no one wanted her. Wherever she went, S.G. Lane met the response that she was overweight and not tall enough.

But Lane was a defiant one—she wanted what she wanted, and she wanted to be a model. She was unwilling to give up her dream. That mind-set ultimately paid off big. When Lane was twenty-one, a photographer came up to her at a party and asked her to pose for him. That was the beginning of Lane's career, and she became a top model. Now in her forties, Lane is still modeling and shows no sign of stopping.

Lane had to love all of herself to radiate the vibe that only ownership can provide. This girl had to fall in love with a very round and voluptuous body to exude the kind of beauty she did. A more traditional skinny model's body just wouldn't have created the same impact. And S.G. Lane was wise enough to know that.

Like Lane, each one of us has to fall in love with something outside the norm to have our beauty. We are all human, so we each have the parts of ourselves that we don't approve of. We must embrace these parts especially to be truly gorgeous. We have to love our strengths and weaknesses to be as attractive as we can be. That is the opportunity, not the burden. The amazing thing is that we can give ourselves an incredible beauty booster simply by changing how we approach our "negative" aspects. Mae West, one of my favorite Sister Goddesses, wrote in *Goodness Had Nothing to Do with It,* "A woman shall resolve as early as possible in life to make the most of whatever delightful natural advantages she may have in the way of face and figure, and resolve never, never to let herself go into slovenly decline. What is important to know is that every woman can have her own kind of beauty, if she's willing to look for it and try for it. Men like so many things."

S.G. Janice did just that. She came to me confessing that she hated her breasts. She was a bodybuilder, and bodybuilders tend to lose a bunch of fat tissue. Janice looked buff, but as she toned and muscled, she lost a lot of fat tissue from her chest. Her breasts, sweethearts though they were, did sag. Janice wanted implants, but Mama beguiled her with a preimplant experiment. I gave her specific instructions: Several times every day, S.G. Janice had to look at her breasts and find something she liked about them. She was forbidden to dwell on what she thought they lacked. She had done enough of that! So, S.G. Janice would stand in front of a mirror, unbuckle her bra, and look at what was *good* about her breasts, not what was wrong, which was her usual custom. S.G. Janice followed this exercise to a T, and guess what? She began to like the nipple color and shape of her breasts, the smooth golden tone of her skin, and the very fact that she *had* breasts.

After only a week of self-approval, Janice was back at the gym when a man she had never spoken to approached her and said, "Excuse me, I feel a little awkward to ask, but did you get a boob job? Your breasts look fabulous." S.G. Janice was shocked—and delighted. She suddenly didn't feel the need for implants anymore.

Now, years later, Janice finds that the lesson she learned from accepting a part of herself that she once hated still sticks. When she is vigilant about her approval of her whole self, Janice loves her body. And when she sinks into the well of disapproval, she hates it. Janice knows that how attractive her body is and how the world responds to it is totally up to her. It's no surprise to me that S.G. Janice's current boyfriend *adores* her breasts. When we claim our beauty, the world follows suit.

Babette, a School of Womanly Arts dropout, embraced the point of view that S.G. Janice ultimately shunned. She accepted the outer world's view of the correct salary, possessions, social life, body, whole existence—instead of creating her own custom version of life and self. Babette had married a rich guy so she could be rich, but she felt poor. She had two kids quickly so she could become a member of garden clubs and children's aid societies, with the hope of being accepted by her affluent New Jersey suburb's community. But she still didn't accept herself. After giving birth to two children, Babette's breasts were a little saggy. In an effort to feel great about her body, this gal went for size C breast implants, liposuction, and Botox.

Now, after all those little operations, she has big breasts, a small waist, and no frown lines. But S.G. Babette still doubts herself, and it shows. She is obsessed, for no reason, with the idea that her rich husband may be having an affair. She is suspicious of all the women he works with. Babette frantically pursues every beauty treatment at the spas in town, not for her pleasure. She throws extravagant parties that she never enjoys just because she feels inadequate. Happiness that is store bought never cuts it.

Those who don't enjoy their own spirit, sensuality, personality, and preferences are never as beautiful as they could be. After all, it's hard to be beautiful when you are teetering about in a state of uncertainty, wondering when the rules are going to change and you are going to be left behind. You need to keep in mind that you are the creatrix. You make the rules, you change the rules, so you are never left behind. Your energy is free to glow all about you and through you because you are the queen of your very own game of life. No spark or sparkle of you is consumed by worry or uncertainty. Everything you are is directed at the next wish or whim or wisdom you decide to pursue.

The most gorgeous woman I know is Dr. Vera Bodansky. She is sixty-five years old, a cancer survivor, and a sex educator. She and her husband, Steve, have Ph.D.'s in sensuality from More University, in California, an institution that researches sensual pleasure. Steve and Vera taught there for twenty years before going out on their own and writing what's now considered *the* book on sexual pleasure, *Extended Massive Orgasm.*

Vera is a woman who revels in her sensuality. When you see Vera, you see radiant womanhood. Her life force, her love of life, is so strong that it just glows all about her. Of course, Vera has signs of aging—she is a grandmother with eight grandchildren—but what you see when you look at her is a dewy beauty. The reason that Vera (and all women with a rich, expansive sensual life) looks fabulous and glows is that those eight thousand clitoral nerve endings get stroked. When the clitoris is happy, there is an awakening in the body and your whole being lights up.

Once you have made the decision to own your beauty, you can get on with your accomplishments. Beauty is power, power we all have at our fingertips. Sister Goddesses take on their beauty, while most women will spend their lives wanting beauty and the rest of life's rich bounty but never feeling they have it. A woman who owns her beauty has the world by the ovaries.

When I was twelve years old and entering the painful awkwardness of adolescence, I saw Barbra Streisand in *Funny Girl.* I watched this movie eighteen times because what I saw before me was the power of a woman's decision to become beautiful, despite her unconventional looks. Even then, Barbra Streisand was on her way to making her life into her own fairy tale, one including the handsome prince. I never forgot the message of that movie, and now I see how all it takes to move dreams into reality is belief. Barbra did it. You can, too.

Check out Diana Vreeland. She said, "Never worry about the facts, just project an image to the public." She sure did that. One American journalist suggested the fashion maven resembled a cigar store wooden Indian. The French designers said she was *jolie/laide,* which means "beautiful/ugly." But Diana wasn't cowed by criticism or labels tossed her way. She was too busy becoming the twentieth century's greatest arbiter of style and elegance. Diana was fashion editor at *Harper's Bazaar* for twenty-five years and editor in chief at *Vogue.* She was original, creative, unconventional, and had the power to make herself into an icon by deciding what was beautiful. Regardless of what others said about her, Diana was always linked with beauty. She wanted to make that connection, and she did.

Every woman is dealt equal cards in the beauty game. We each have the same number of votes. We don't all behave as if we have a vote, but the only thing that actually matters in the world of beauty is that we cast our ballot for ourselves. The big truth of the matter is that other people's opinions are virtually immaterial. Comments aimed at us sometimes work as a temporary measure to buoy our confidence higher, like a life preserver when we are drowning. But other people's take on us has no real lasting impact, positive or negative, except for the value we place on it. Once again, we are the vote casters. The sad thing is, most women aren't aware of this.

S.G. Terri and I were chatting one day and she revealed to me that she never felt pretty. She felt fat, dumpy, and unattractive her whole life. She had been looking through an old photo album and came across some pictures of herself as an adolescent and young woman. She was shocked by how beautiful she was. "What a waste!" she said. "I wish I had known I was that good-looking!" It seems like so many women have this same experience sometime in their late twenties, thirties, or forties—they look back at photos of themselves when they were kids or teens or in their early twenties and say, "What was I thinking? I wasn't ugly, I was gorgeous. If only I had known, I would have enjoyed that time so much more!"

So what I'm saying, my darlings, is that with a little work we can all see ourselves as the knockouts we are. Since it is a habit to find yourself unbeautiful, it takes a effort to add on the habit of finding yourself beautiful. Let me explain why I refer to the change that you want to effect as "adding on." It is easier to add a good habit to one's life than to discontinue a bad one. Why? Think about it for a moment. Isn't it much more difficult to say *no* to yourself than *yes* to yourself? I think so. The only way I got over nail-biting was with the treat of weekly manicures. If I stop my manicures, I'm back to nail gnawing. And I'm not the only one who seems to feel this way. One of my S.G.'s recently lost a lot of weight rather easily. Her method was adding on exercise and adding on "crunchy chews"—bags of carrots and celery and other vegetables that she would snack on all day—to her daily habits. This S.G. told me that she owes her success to adding on, rather than subtracting from her life. This makes sense to me. We are greedy—more feels a lot better than less.

Aside from adding on a manicure to cure my nail-biting, I observed others around me to enhance my overall beauty habits. I am forty-five years old and of average looks, but I have turned myself into an astonishingly sexy babe, simply because I wanted to. The same possibility is available to you. I transformed myself by merely observing women who were beautiful in different areas and making their habits my own. I noticed that women who struck me as beautiful and sexy held themselves differently than I did. It was almost as if they were on display. The toss of the hair, the erectness of the posture, the lounging on the furniture, the graceful hand gestures they used all said, "Look at me, I'm so gorgeous!" I became adept at these postures and gestures and I noticed that they actually felt really good and kind of glamorous. These simple moves helped me start thinking of myself as beautiful—it was the "Act as if" principle in effect. I acted as if I were beautiful, and lo and behold, I became that in my eyes and the eyes of others.

I had the luck of overhearing some women's comments about me that led me to believe my mission to become a babe was a success. About eight years ago, I was leading a course and a woman leaned over to the friend beside her and said, while pointing at me, "You know, she is not beautiful, but she acts as though she is." Then I knew I was on my way.

Later, when I met Vera, I realized the secret to her beauty was that she's on intimate terms with her ecstasy. I have noticed that when people are really enjoying themselves, really and truly ecstatic, they are all beautiful. I decided I wanted to learn to come so I could own that part of my existence and beauty as well. Vera and Steve taught me how, and now I teach other women how to get that special glow.

S.G. Lane and other beauties who have taken my courses have also helped me add on to my beauty. I noticed that Lane had everything she touched rise up to her level of loveliness—her accessories, the dishes she served on, the sheets she slept on. I began to redesign my life so that everything I touch, from my sleek cell phone and beautiful wallet to the creams in my bathroom, the shoes in my closet, the champagne flutes in my cupboard, all reflect my beauty. Everything does not have to be expensive—simply deliberate, thoughtful, and conscious.

What I have come to see is that we can embrace our beauty in countless ways. All we have to do is look around and do our best to incorporate our vision of it in every move we make, every item we surround ourselves with, every thought and feeling we have about ourselves and our place in the big, beautiful world around us. Let's take over the world of beauty and make it our own. Let's have our way with beauty and learn how to rejoice and honor that spark of a miracle which we all are born with. Every baby is beautiful. Every woman is beautiful. Every creation of the Goddess is beautiful.

Everyone has times and places in their lives that leave them feeling beautiful. When is it for you? Is it after great sex? When you get your hair done? After a workout? After a massage? If you begin to identify these areas, you can expand them. S.G. Marlene always felt beautiful after she got her hair blown out. Her Sister Goddess friends advised her to get these blowouts twice a week instead of once in a while, and her appreciation of her beauty began to deepen and expand. For S.G. Fanny it's as simple as reaching into her purse and having the whole purse organized and the accessories "just so."

I have created a group of exercises that can help you generate the feeling and experience of beauty in and around you. These work perfectly—as long as you do them. To be their most productive, these activities must, in fact, become your new habits. Come on, my Goddesses, rip off a hunk of beauty for yourselves and parade it around for all to see. If you rise to the challenge of finding and treating yourself like the profound beauty you are, you will not only reap the rewards all babes do but also inspire others around you to do the same. By beautifying yourself and pussifying your life, you will be doing your part to improve the world! Lead your own beauty revolution!

Exercise 1: You Are Cinderella and Her Fairy Godmother

Each of us has areas of our life and experience that we want but we hold back on, often telling ourselves we can't have it because we are not "beautiful" enough. It's time to blast through that barrier, my lovelies. And with this exercise you can do just that. Answer this question, on paper: "How would my life be different if I were beautiful?" Make your list and, perhaps, share it with a girlfriend. Have at least five to twenty things on your list. You will be surprised at the revelations that surface for you. One S.G. said that if she were beautiful, she would be nicer to her husband. Another single S.G. said she could pick up any guy she wanted. Perhaps for you it's a raise, or a new apartment, or great sex. See what's on the list, and then you can decide if you want to move on any of those goals NOW.

Exercise 2: How to Talk to Yourself

At least three times a day, every day, say out loud to yourself, "I am beautiful." You can say this life-changing little phrase as you walk down the street, as you pass a mirror, at your desk. You can quietly think, "I am beautiful," as many times a day as you wish, but you must say it out loud no less than three times. For extra credit, do it in front of a mirror and give yourself a little wink as you do. This exercise totally changes your body chemistry from self-negation to self-adoration in one second flat. If you do it before an important meeting or dinner with your boyfriend, you are a genius! You don't need to worry about changing the unconscious messages you send yourself every day; they'll start changing on their own once you convince yourself of your gorgeousness. Just add on this little ditty and you will be giving yourself a three-second beauty treatment every time you do!

Exercise 3: Redecorate Your External Landscape

Get in there, take over, and glorify your closet. Create space in your life for beauty. Keep only clothing that you feel absolutely beautiful in. Get rid of anything that you have doubts about. Give it away to charity or to a girlfriend. Organize that underwear drawer. Throw out those shoes that don't fit, that costume jewelry you never wear.

I did this exercise with Auntie Beth last year. We dumped twenty bags of has-beens from my wardrobe. The stuff was OK—it just wasn't sexy or beautiful enough. I was left with about five items in my closet. Once I made this move, the most wonderful thing happened—some designers started giving me clothes, a dear girlfriend bought me a fantastic coat and boots. Before my very eyes, my closet started to fill with lovely little numbers without any effort or money on my part. Now my wardrobe is worthy of me for the first time in my life, and getting better. The same thing can happen to you. All you have to do is trust that the power of desire in action, combined with the power of owning your beauty, will make you an unstoppable bombshell. How can you say *no* to that? Go for it, gals!

Exercise 4: Make Every Meal Fit for a Queen—You!

The act of glorifying your life makes you feel good as you move through different moments of your day. When you reach in your closet for something to wear and everything is delectable, you instantly feel wonderful, and you look even more wonderful because of the pleasure your life, in its details, brings you.

Take this lesson to the kitchen and to the table. When you eat, make sure it is exactly what you wish and that you draw it toward you in the grand style, fit for a queen. If it is a potato chip, have it on your favorite piece of china. If it is cottage cheese, eat it out of your crystal bowl. You get the idea—no stuff-and-shove. Only giving yourself the full richness of your desires on a platter will do, and relish every bite. You are the queen of your desires and your world—so act like one, especially when you are the only one there to see it. You deserve the best. Accept nothing less.

Exercise 5: Redecorate Your Internal Landscape

Many S.G.'s have found power and peace through accepting beauty into their lives. Can you think of a ritual that might make your life more beautiful? For one S.G. it was as simple as lighting all the candles in her apartment; buying a loaf of bread, a hunk of cheese, some wine; and then sitting on the floor, naked, in front of her mirror. She then read herself a poem entitled "Love After Love" by Derek Walcott.

Be willing to celebrate the beauty in you with poetry, dance, and song. Become expert at finding beauty in every aspect of womanhood, fat or thin, young or ancient, petite or imposing. S.G. Paula won the S.G. of the Week award once because she used to be such a snob about beauty but after taking the course she found that her willingness to accept more of herself had led to her feeling a sense of sisterhood with all women—especially women of different classes, races, backgrounds, and education. In finding herself, she found the tissue that connects all women.

Exercise 6: Falling in Love with Yourself

Write yourself a love letter. Sit at your desk with flowers, candles. Put on great music. Set the mood—as though you were your lover writing a love letter to you. Read it out loud. None of us spend nearly enough time owning our greatness, or praising our gorgeous fabulousness. In the first place, it's really fun to do. Second, it has amazing consequences in the world. S.G. Ruth wrote herself the sexiest, most gushy, romantic love letter of her class. She was shocked when, two weeks later, her boyfriend, Ernest, spontaneously wrote her his first love letter. The eerie thing was that the way he praised her was so similar to her own self-celebration, it was as if he had read her thoughts. Hey, if a guy's gonna read your thoughts, you might as well have yummy ones!

Lesson 7

The Womanly Art of Partying with Your Inner Bitch

Don't talk to me about rules, dear. Wherever I stay, I make the goddamn rules.

—Maria Callas

Your mission, should you choose to accept it, is to sink down with me, twenty thousand leagues under the sea, to dive for the pearls most valuable and difficult to attain. They are located way down in you, hidden within your dark side. You comin'? A moment of hesitation is normal, but I hope you can bully through it and follow me, darlings. If you do, you will take another huge step toward a fun and fulfilling existence.

Our dark side is a part of ourselves we feel uncomfortable owning. It's easy for us to be effective, talented, pretty, charismatic, reliable, attentive, and supportive. But we don't feel so good about showing disapproval or disagreement, our hurt, anger, or vulnerability. All that is part of the dark side. And to make the most of our best, bright, jewel-like qualities, we must first venture into our darkest emotions. We cannot always be the good girl and still be able to tap into the amazing power of our individual enthusiasm, love, and fun.

Yes, my courageous ones, being a Sister Goddess means approving of every facet of the Goddess within you, not just the good and happy parts. In fact, the more you develop a rapport with your dark side, the more truly happy and balanced you will be. The womanly art I'd like you to learn is how to form bonds of friendship, love, and understanding with all your shortcomings, downfalls, or weaknesses. It's time to get closely acquainted with your hellion's rage, your bottomless sadness, your spiny jealousy, your deep greed, and your profound loneliness.

You might be asking yourself, "Why must we take this dark trip?" There is a very good reason, indeed. We women are currently all living in a cloud of repressed emotion—mostly anger, from what I can see. You know how I know women are angry? They get angry as soon as you suggest they might be angry. This is because many women spend their whole lives trying to act nice, and when that nice cover is busted, all the anger they have been storing, along with frustration at their inability to completely hide it, comes right to the surface. I also know from personal experience how anger can be pushed down for years, and the toll such suppression can take.

I suffered from a case of anger from the age of twelve until I was well into my thirties. Only when I looked back from a new perspective of fulfillment and fun did I see the festering that had filled my life. I was angry at the spiritual, physical, and educational consequences of being a girl. I felt alienated, lonely, ungrateful, exiled, and disgusted. I managed these feelings—not by expressing them but by internalizing them. I became sullen and moody. I overate, bit my nails, and underachieved like a master.

It wasn't until years later, when I began to have a sense of my own rightness and began to explore the world of pleasure, that I felt righteous about my anger and free to use it constructively. Anger is like a machete. If I directed it toward my goals, I could hack a pathway through the brambles of life like nothing else. If I directed it toward myself or a loved one, it could cause serious if not fatal injury. It was downright pathetic to see how, for years, my internalized anger whittled my life down to a sliver of what it could have been.

A woman's anger, righteously channeled, is an invaluable tool. Today so many women are simmering close to a boil, though we, agreeable as we often are, may not always acknowledge it.

These are times of great change, and of conflicting and seldom-met expectations. Women have more opportunity and freedom than ever before, but we're still raised to subordinate our desires to those of others around us, and have little experience in identifying and going for our own. The changing social and economic landscape offers us lots of different possibilities, but often we don't move ahead with what we really want. We just kind of put our lives on one track—the career track, the mommy track, the unhappy track—and go.

Ultimately, automatic pilot doesn't get us very far. We are angry when our lives don't end up looking like the fairy tale we were raised to expect. We grow up, enter the workforce, and tell ourselves that independence is great. But on some level we are still waiting for a prince to carry us off to his castle, even if we earn twice as much as the prince does; and if we do, that makes us mad, too. We are also angry when our lives end up looking like the fairy tale. Some prince shows up and expects us to leave our fabulous life, join him in his, make his dinner and his babies, and keep his household . . . I don't think so! Being responsible for work and household and child rearing all at once makes us mad. Having no man and no kid can piss a gal right off, too.

Oh, these are testy times, testy times to be with a man or without one. We all judge ourselves so harshly. I think that is the worst of it—our judgment of ourselves. We think we are wrong if we are not rich or married or both by the time we are thirty. It's only anger at our own selves that gives us so little elasticity, so little humor or resilience when someone else disapproves of us. We women all have a little tiny fuse, and when it blows, we are angry, defensive, bitter, and confused. The only way out of this dilemma is for us gals individually to decide what we want, and go for it. I'm not saying the path you choose for yourself will be easily trod, but at least you have a chance to get what you really want for your trouble.

So, one of the main things we can do to come out of the fray holding what we want is to really get in touch with our individual desires. Anger can help us do this. Anger is often a big signpost that points us toward areas in our lives where we feel shortchanged. Once we locate those hot spots of anger or resentment or sadness, or just the ache of want, we can start asking ourselves what would fill those spaces and what steps should be taken first.

In what areas are you a slave to your life? Are you a slave to fashion? Your husband? Your children? Your job? You will be amazed to see how many areas you can name, once you set your mind to it. Are you a slave to youth? A slave to money? To time? Are you too scared to get the job you want? Too resigned to tell your husband exactly what you want in bed? Do you submit to the expectations of others?

To compromise? Until we know what's got us under its thumb, we can't choose an alternative. Identifying those things that currently rule your world and limit you is a crucial step.

Mama's goal here is simply to expose where we are so we focus our energy in a more positive direction, namely toward our pleasure. That is the choice: anger versus pleasure. We have the freedom to choose. Our pent-up anger is a wonderful turbo boost, but it can also bring about great damage if it's left to boil and embitter us. Mama wants you to practice the art of using your anger for your own benefit, rather than suffer behind it. You have a rich emotional terrain, teeming with energy, passion, and life. Mama wants you to mine this fertile soil without getting blown up by anger's land mines.

When we women do not admit we are angry, when we do not admit we are at war, then the whole world becomes our battle zone. If it is never unbottled, our anger gets expressed in subversive ways. S.G. Catherine is one gal who comes to mind when I think about what happens when anger isn't released constructively. She was so angry at her workaholic husband, Steven, that she would rack up thousands upon thousands of dollars of unnecessary expenses just to drive him through the roof. Catherine never thought to simply ask Steven for more time and attention. All she knew and acted upon was that he paid attention to her when the American Express bill came. This kind of personal battle is a little like the war in Vietnam—it goes on for decades, nobody wins, and in the end you forget why you were fighting.

Unfocused, floating anger is not educational. It is not enlightening. It is only destructive. S.G. Catherine eventually saw that, by giving herself the attention she craved first, she was able to show Steven that a better balance of work and play (especially play with Catherine) would bring them both more happiness and success. He never heard this request when she screamed at him. He heard it only when she was calm and gratified enough to communicate in a friendly manner. Once Catherine was able to get the edge off her anger, she was able to change her life with her husband into the one they both enjoyed.

Part of being a Sister Goddess is allowing yourself to feel the way you feel. Feel the whole thing—the whole rage, the whole fear, the whole loneliness. Invite it into yourself, don't shy away from it. When your feelings start flowing, stand in the face of their full power and rejoice. Rage! Cry or rant! Have the feelings that you have. It is important to understand that your feelings are right. Your passion is part of your genius.

Sometimes an S.G. won't feel so secure at first, in expressing her anger. S.G. Barbara was one of my goddesses who was hesitant at first to step up and accept her angry feelings toward her boyfriend of two years, Tom, and her roommate, Linda. What happened was that Barbara and Tom often went out and took Linda with them. Linda was single, and Tom and Linda got along great. In fact, soon they were a little too chummy for S.G. Barbara's comfort. At first Barbara just sulked and moped. Then, when she got Tom alone, she cried to him about her insecurities and her suspicions about Linda. Well, how totally lame. How completely unconstructive. A few weeks into her Womanly Arts classes, Barbara began to feel right about her anger, right about her comfort zone with Linda and Tom, and right about putting the kibosh on behavior that displeased her. So, what did she do? Barbara told Linda to cool her jets with Tom and get her own boyfriend.

Like Barbara, women who feel out of control over their messiest emotions do not get their way. They become part of the guerrilla force of angry women, using their biological power in subversive ways.

However, when Barbara laid down the law, the war was over and she was able to resume her friendship with Linda. Once the issue between them was out in the open, Barbara felt respected and strong, and Linda gave her friend credit for standing up for how she felt.

When we feel powerless, disenchanted, and generally unfulfilled, women will sneak around on one another. We will take what's not nailed down, claw our way to the top. We will practice a little back-stabbing before lunch, and a bit of backbiting after tea. Hey—we are not gentlemen. We are lustful, lascivious, hungry guests at the banquet of life. Most of us have never permitted ourselves a proper seat at the banquet table. We have been the servers and the greeters and the coat-check girls—grabbing a little of what we can as we go. In order to take a rightful seat at the head of the banquet table of our lives, we have to accept the rightness of our feelings and desires and act on them strongly, always.

Most of us women are furious at men whether we know it or not. We're so angry at being ignored and passed over and diminished that we would shoot a hole through the rowboat of life and go down with the ship, just for the pleasure of watching the guy sitting next to us get what's coming to him. Guys wouldn't do this. When they finally did notice that the boat they were in was sinking, they would make sure the little woman got the life vest, first. After all, any man in such a boat wouldn't have generations of anger, frustration, and disappointment fueling that little self-destructive act, as a woman would.

When faced with anger or despair, our most elegant option is to rise above the problem and put our life energy into something way more fun. That is what S.G. Emma found out. S.G. Emma's boyfriend of fifteen years, John, broke up with her. This was his idea—he felt too young to be in a committed relationship, too young to be tied down.

When John told her that it was over between them, S.G. Emma was furious, then distraught. She had been in love with John and wanted to marry him. So she went to therapy. What she found there was a chance to look at what was wrong with her and John, and how she had intimacy issues and stuff with her past she hadn't handled. The therapy approach didn't help S.G. Emma's mood at all, so when she heard from a friend about my classes, she decided to attend.

When Emma came to her first Womanly Arts class, she found out that Mama had a different solution. After asking a few questions I discovered that Emma's whole life with John had revolved around John. (And I don't have to tell you how common this orbit mentality is among women. I know you have girlfriends whose significant other is the center of their universe, girlfriends who feel lost in space. The problem is, the biggest loser in this scenario, even when their partner is around, is them.) My first move was to get Emma to go out and have way more fun than she had been having. And to her credit, Emma did splendidly. She started dating other guys, doing volunteer work, and hanging out with her girlfriends.

As a consequence of expanding her life, Emma had more fun and became more fun to be with. She looked better than ever and she was enjoying the attention she was getting from her new guys. S.G. Emma vowed to me and the other Goddesses in her class that she would never go back to stepping, fetching, cleaning, and cooking to keep her man. It was way too much work, and it did not lead Emma to her goal of having a great sexy partnership with a guy.

Well, S.G. Emma's positive experience from pleasure wasn't over yet. Sensing the fun, John came back, sniffing around the much more interesting and exciting S.G. Emma. Emma was pleased (who wouldn't be with a guy slinking back?) and started seeing John, but she continued along with the other guys. S.G. Emma's got a whole new take on the situation now. She's enjoying John's company, but Emma's not even sure if she wants to marry him anymore. She is sure that fun has made a difference in her confidence, her communication, and her experience.

Like S.G. Emma, S.G. Laura, an accountant, also found a way to drop anger in favor of fun. Before she joined Mama Gena, Laura was tight-lipped and cooperative around her colleagues in her firm. She was the only woman in a sea of men and secretly thought her colleagues all worked too hard and shouldn't take on every case that came their way. She felt overworked and isolated, and she was pissed. However, after starting the class, S.G. Laura began to exert her Goddessliness over the office. She would ask the guys to do things for her that she didn't like doing. She had them hire an extra accountant to help with her load. She suggested they accept only clients they were enthusiastic about, and was surprised to find all of her suggestions were met with great appreciation. She had been so terrified of being shot down or criticized, it took everything S.G. Laura had to loosen her lips and add her point of view to the meetings. Until Laura got up the courage to voice her valuable opinions, her colleagues had no idea she was sitting on a gold mine of viewpoints that could enhance their business and make it a more pleasurable daily experience.

Like many women, S.G. Laura had grown up with the directive "Be nice." "Don't say what you feel or what you want, especially if it might disturb something or someone." I refer to this as the Barbie/Disney mind-set. When we agree to be polite and decorative, we do not live the full range of female experience. If we feel acceptable only as a Barbie/Disney girl, we are going to live a very limited, Barbie/Disney life, where everything is blandly pretty and happy (or is sure to end up that way). If we don't reject the Barbie/Disney model we will never know our full brilliance or our darkest, ink-black depths. Yes, we are back to the lair of the bitch Goddess. Welcome home!

I would be nothing without my dark side. My rage, when used lovingly, is one of the most effective tools I have in my toolbox. Besides my anger there is my greed—my vast, lusty greediness. Without it, I would not have my town house, my beach house, my jewels, my fur, my designer clothes, all of which I cherish. I have to mention my lust—my raw outrageous lust, which I would overcome any obstacle to gratify. Why, that is my greatest gift of all. My raw lustiness has led to my sweetest memories—kisses so light, barely tasted, kisses so still and so deep they touched eternity.

I believe that greed can be used for the good of all. I let nothing stand in the way of my desires. My desires have always led me, and my husband, friends, and family, to more joy. Greed isn't necessarily a character flaw. I believe that we are all essentially moral and generous. We behave badly only when we are profoundly ungratified. If you put a starved person at a banquet table, it would be inhumane and unrealistic to ask them to leave most of what's there for others. By the same token, women are so starved for attention, sensual gratification, and the lifestyle they crave that they will seize it desperately in almost any form.

In many cases we women don't know our bottomless pits have a bottom. We think we won't get another chance to fill up our aching need again, so when we begin to get to know what our desires are, we can get grabby with the good stuff that comes our way. When we get just a taste of what pleases us deeply, we can feel out of control.

How do you get control of yourself? The answer: Serve your lust. Bow to it at all costs. Fill yourself up—yes, even at the expense of other people, if you must. Once you learn to feel satiated you can even open doors for others to find their way to bounty. An unfulfilled woman can't expect to live on the moral high ground, she will forgo all scruples to satisfy her hunger for pleasure. Be forewarned, however: bowing to your lust will bring happiness, but it requires rising above the guilt.

Sister Goddess Shawn was one of those gals men learned to avoid. She had met Kevin, a wealthy man she had targeted as daddy material, and when she got what she wanted—a baby—she divorced him. When Mama met her, Shawn admitted that she felt wrong about marrying for money and a baby, and wrong about her divorce, which left her child without a father at home. As a result, she kept forcing whoever she was dating to be a dad and that backfired every time.

You might think that men left Shawn because they didn't want to be thrust into the daddy role, but the truth is, it was because Shawn couldn't bear to admit what she really wanted. What Shawn really wanted—something she admitted several weeks into her first Womanly Arts class—was to be supported by her ex-husband; to share custody of their son, David, so that three nights a week she could go out and dance and have fun with her friends; to go back to school; and to date any guy she wished. Shawn felt she was asking for too much.

Ultimately, Shawn not only suggested shared custody but asked Kevin to pay for her school tuition so she could get the education she needed to support herself and her child. He agreed! Turns out that Kevin wanted the mother of his son to be self-reliant. He adores David and wants him to have all the advantages—even the advantage of a flourishing mom. Miraculously, Kevin even agreed to pay Shawn's rent and expenses while she finished school. Shawn was so grateful and happy to have Kevin's total support, and even more pleased she had the courage to go for what she wanted.

The upshot of all of this is that when a woman goes for and gets what she wants, everyone is happy. Shawn really got to let loose in the fun department, she no longer had to find a guy to stuff into a daddy suit, and she found she was enjoying the men she was dating for the first time in her life. And she had more men interested in her than ever! Similarly, Kevin was happy that those closest to him—Shawn and David—were finally happy. He was able to help raise his son and remain the loving man he always was. David now has a great relationship with his mom and his dad, both of whom adore him. None of this could have happened for Shawn and Kevin and David if they were a traditional, nuclear family. Our great responsibility, and the only path to our happiness, is to define what we want our life to be and go after that with a vengeance. Tradition be damned.

I think the biggest challenge for an S.G. is to find the parts of herself that she is hiding and surrender to them. Anger is a huge territory that most women have not explored, but envy, greed, lust, and fear can also reside in our dark side. Fear is perhaps the most insidious of all. Back in the old days of being an actress, in my years of college through age thirty-two or so, I did not lack talent. I was actually the best actress I had ever seen. I had it all—I looked good, sang, had an ear for dialects, flawless timing, and huge range—the whole package. But I had something even greater than my talent that always stood in my way. My fear of my talent. I had way more of *that* than anything. And I was familiar with fear—it was an old coat, and I recognized its smell. When I was wearing that old rag I was safe.

I was safe from being observed and held accountable for being glorious. I can remember writing a letter to a favorite director and theater company owner, saying I could not return for another season for a part they had offered me. There were other things that were more pressing in my life. Guess what they were? Staying in New York, going to therapy, and taking acting classes. I couldn't possibly fit a potentially life-changing acting role into my schedule. The part was Celia in *As You Like It,* at a fantastic theater company in the Berkshires. It would have been my big break.

As time went on and I grew older, I went further and further into hiding, compiling great lists of reasons why I could not move forward in my career, or my relationships, or my happiness. And the kerflooey part is that I would defend my inertia with such great conviction. I was so certain that the action I was taking was absolutely the right one for me.

S.G. Lisa was another one who couldn't embrace her own greatness. She was basically donating her time to the Wall Street firm where she worked. S.G. Lisa felt so ill equipped to ask for money that she never did. Perceiving a lack of ambition, the partners in her firm gave her less and less responsibility over time. When she came to Mama, S.G. Lisa had just received a $20,000-a-year pay cut.

Another Sister Goddess was a fantastically talented painter and potter. She had spent the last twenty years in New York City doing temp jobs (twenty years of temping!), complaining about not having any time for her art, and all the while her parents were paying her rent so she could afford to keep temping. This one also made it a habit of never dating *anyone* she could bring home to Mama. All of the men she chose to see were twenty years younger, or had a negligible grasp of the English language, or were alcoholic or in love with some other woman.

Phew! These examples always get me. You can just see how the fear of accomplishing anything, let alone our big dreams, can keep us hogtied for years. I think women are susceptible to this debilitating condition because it's so easy to listen to the little voice of doubt that whispers, "You are not beautiful enough," "You are not smart enough," "You are just not good enough." Women get a little shook up in my classes at first because they've been downright comfortable with their diminished view of themselves. The Goddess is aching to put women in their rightful place on the throne of possibility. However, getting from that comfortable spot on the floor to that stage of unlimited potential is a challenge.

Many women are so terribly scared to experience their full emotional, spiritual, and sexual range because they are intimidated by their own innate power. If you have never let yourself fully sob your eyes out, you will be scared that such an unchecked torrent of tears may engulf and overwhelm you. If you have never let your rage out of the bag, you are probably afraid to let it explode, for fear it will irreparably harm or destroy you. If you have never really learned to come, you will feel scared that your bottled-up sensuality will overtake you and obliterate everything except your raw, hungry, throbbing desire. If you have never played full-out and failed, you won't want to leap into the game, any game, for fear you will not survive a misstep.

Mama wants to invite you into your fear. Your fear is your gift. Like anger, it acts like the internal marker to your own magnificence. Now, you are going to be scared when you first step off the well-trod path and start skittering across the ice of your brilliance. Take the appearance of fear as a very positive sign. For fear does not visit when you are conforming and safely following the rules. Often fear is an indicator that you are onto something good, something really valuable. You can train yourself to welcome fear to your table, invite it in from the cold. Go ahead and twirl with it, darlings. Since the fear isn't going to vanish, learn to boogie with it.

The only way out of your fears is through them. They will always greet you, whether you're giving birth, starting your own business, making a painting, or falling in love. But those who wow us with their creativity and daring know the fear tends to ease once you accept it. Madonna, for example, likes to pick the thing she is the most scared of, and lunge for it. For her most recent album and concert tour, she is accompanying herself on the guitar. Madonna doesn't *have* to do that. She's a great singer and dancer and entertainer. But Madonna has learned to use her fear to spur her creativity. Nothing and no one gets created without some element of fear. Everything worthwhile in life involves some tremor caused by the unknown, the as yet unexperienced.

S.G. Carmen learned this when she went on a recent job interview. She was very nervous about negotiating for this position. She knew these potential employers were going to offer her $70,000, which she was willing to take, but she wondered if she should ask for more. Mama's policy is, ask for a sum that scares you. If it doesn't scare you, it's not enough. We women are comfortable with "a little less." Let's make ourselves uncomfortable, with "a little more." Why should Tom Cruise or Harrison Ford make more than Julia Roberts?

I gave this talk to S.G. Carmen and urged her to go for more. She was excited by the challenge and practiced asking for $90,000 at the interview. Guess what happened? S.G. Carmen was rewarded for her daring. And how thrilled was she when she got the job offer with a salary she was not sure she could get? She was giddy with delight, my darlings! Settling is not as much fun as going for it, so why not go for it?

S.G. Joy is another woman who was limiting herself, who had to work to accept the potential she carried within her. She was raised in a conservative household and thought women should *never* ask a guy out. From what I could see, Joy was a come-hither type but she was thirty and never had a boyfriend that she was really crazy about. All that changed after she met Mama. Then she was in Aspen, at a bar, and she saw a really cute guy. He wasn't noticing her, he was absorbed in thought. But being the recent Womanly Arts School graduate that she was, S.G. Joy decided to do something she had never done before—she went over to the guy and said, "Hi! What's your name?" Do you have any doubt that our gal got the guy? Doubt no more—S.G. Joy and Rob have been dating for two months.

Now, getting the job, the salary, and the guy is what Mama considers a small but significant victory. You have to battle your everyday garden-variety terror before you reach it. Then there is the deeper, the more serious kind of fear diving, that happens when you risk offending the status quo to create a selfishly pleasurable lifestyle. The higher the form of gratification, the greater the fear at the outset. Whenever you are taking on huge life challenges, facing existential fear, take it head-on and see what happens. If you are currently encountering real terror, I say, rejoice! Chances are your future is just about to get really exciting, and to provide you with pleasures you scarcely thought possible.

You don't have to race and burst through your fears all at one time. If you keep up your pleasure exercises from the previous lessons, you will find that you are becoming more open and outgoing, more lively and sassy, more courageous and unstoppable than perhaps you ever thought you could be. This, my darlings, is just the beginning! Let me show you techniques that will help you tame those few lingering, beastly fears. Be ready for a big change in your world—be prepared to seize more exhilarating opportunities than you have ever imagined! They are soon to be yours.

Exercise 1: The Letter

Write a letter to someone you are angry at. Get everything off your chest. The goal of this exercise is to let you see that your rage or anger is not random—it is very specific. It has a bottom, it can be expressed and dissipated. I do not recommend sending your rage letter. Just focus on writing it, that's the liberating part.

After you have written this letter reread it a week or two later to see if there is anything that you would still like to express on the subject of your letter. Your goal could be to make contact and communicate with him/her/them *without* the anger. Anger inhibits communication. If you find you are still too angry to speak calmly to whoever inspired your letter, do the next exercise—Spring Cleaning—in order to dissipate what's left of your anger. Then put the letter in a drawer. Pull it out a week later. If the negative charge *still* hasn't diminished, start writing again. Take this opportunity to really hold forth—list everything you wish you could actually say. Describe their transgressions, their limitations, their inadequacies. Be vicious, be vile. Get it all out. Make it worse than it truly is! Do not hold out! After all your anger is accounted for on paper and set away in a drawer, allow yourself to put it to rest.

Exercise 2: Spring Cleaning—Anger

The goal of this exercise is to clean your closet of any old dust balls of anger, resentment, or rage you have hanging out in there, taking up valuable space. This exercise clears out all those old feelings so you can open up to new, more fun ones. You can do this exercise alone or with a partner.

Spring Cleaning, Alone

An S.G. sits by herself and does this process aloud. She questions herself, and then answers herself.

For example:

S.G. asks:	What do you have on "anger"? (This question is always the same, and asked in a simple, expressionless way.)
S.G. answers (for example):	I am angry at my mother.
S.G. says:	Thank you (simple, expressionless way, not robotic).

In place of the word "anger," you can substitute someone you are actually angry at, like your mom or your boyfriend or your boss. Do this exercise for fifteen minutes. Do the cycle over and over again.

You can do this with a partner, with one S.G. asking the question over and over and the other S.G. answering. The exercise is to be totally confidential. Each person does it for fifteen minutes, then switches.

Exercise 3: The Gift

Send an anonymous gift to someone you hate. See how it makes you feel. Do you still hate them? Or do you like them more? This is one of my favorite exercises, because it is so unexpected. We think of gift giving when we like someone, not when we dislike them or are angry at them. But when you give someone a gift, you actually start to like them more. It feels good to like people—it feels a lot better than disliking them. You can actually begin to like someone when you get a gift for them. I had S.G.'s do this in a course once and it was one of the most favorite and fun parts of the class. This group got to be so close because they managed their negative charge with gift giving.

Exercise 4: The Poem

Write your own rage mantra or rage poem. Focus on expressing angry thoughts and feelings about your anger on paper and take notice of any clarifying and healing effects. When I do this exercise, I feel an incredible release, and a wave of relaxation envelops me. Does this happen to you? Or is there something else you feel? Do this exercise as many times as you like.

To get you started, I'll share with you poems other Sister Goddesses have written. One S.G. taking my course stated in her anger poem, entitled "If She Loved Her Anger More," that "she would wrap herself around [her anger] and let it be the rocket that propels her." Another S.G., in a piece entitled "Rage of the Goddess Soiree Poem: Celebrating My Anger," spoke of "wiping the taint off rage and letting it soar free." See what kind of emotion your words can set free.

Exercise 5: Reread Lesson 4

Exercise 6: Do Something Every Day That Scares You

Notice your fears. Are you scared of commitment? Scared of changing careers? Scared of telling your husband or best friend the truth? Scared of auditioning? Having a baby?

This exercise is not about biting off the whole enchilada. It's about taking small steps in the direction of your fears. You are afraid of buying your first house or apartment? Just go house hunting. Scared of dating? Tag along with some girlfriends as they go to parties or out with guy friends. Scared of having a baby? Just go get a checkup at your gynecologist's. Baby steps toward your dreams get you there just as efficiently as great leaps.

* * *

Are you charged by the adventure? Are you ready to toss off some fear, my dears? Remember, anger and other negative emotions aren't bad any more than a thunderstorm is bad—once you get your foul-weather gear and rain boots on, you get to splash in the puddles. C'mon, follow Mama and I'll lead the way.

Lesson 8

The Womanly Art of Owning and Operating Men

A woman serves a man best when she has her joy above all other values.
—Dr. Victor Baranco

Getting with the program of self-fulfillment and adding a partner to the mix isn't always easy. It never has been, and as the pace of modern life speeds ever faster, you may feel that trying to get some satisfaction is like trying to catch a train that's moving at the speed of light. Gender games are constantly evolving. You never know if you're measuring up to old standards, or unaware of new rules, or about to be disappointed, or creating circumstances you just don't know how to deal with, or heading for results you never anticipated.

We keep on trying because—what else can we do? We don't want to be lonely, unfulfilled, empty, and sad. We want to find love. So we keep working to get our relationships right. But as everyone already knows, however much we add to our lives, our relationships will never bring us complete fulfillment. We have to look to ourselves for that. Usually it's when we delight in our own selves that we attract others to us.

If you think that a man is going to lead you to your true happiness, you are all drunk—drunk, I tell you. Drunk on the legend of Sleeping Beauty, Cinderella, Snow White. Well, I'll say it again, 'cause I can't say it enough—that wait for Mr. Right is gonna keep your life and happiness on hold as long as it exists. Get a grip, girls. Those fairy tales you were raised on were Grimm indeed. Kiss your own self and wake your own self up from centuries of slumber. When you wait for that prince and give him your magic wand of happiness, you can mix and match what you get—divorce, low self-esteem, low libido, health problems, prescriptions for Lopressor and Prozac, or just really long cocktail hours that work to anesthetize you further so you can handle how much you have anesthetized yourself already. You won't be able to handle the fact that none of your desires are being met. To be met, your desires must have the power of *you* behind them. Sure, it's great if your man is backing your action, but you have to lead the way. You and you alone!

How are you doing with your relationships with men? Proud? Happy? Fulfilled? Pleased with your womanly self? If so, GREAT! You are among the satisfied minority. Most of the women I meet have a complaint list about men that's longer than their desire list. Some suffer from see-men-ophobia. Scream-menitis. No-menomania. Others have just gone off the deep end and become raging lunatics who blame men for the lack of love, romance, respect, and great sex in their lives. Well, I'll tell you, just as I tell them, don't blame your man, ladies. Once again, the responsibility for your pleasure is yours—not theirs.

So many of us come to the man/woman game looking for Mr. Perfect. We dismiss guys who aren't rich enough, or smart enough, or fill-in-the-blank enough. There's always something. And many of us who settle down with Mr. Good Enough miss the happily-ever-after because we never admit to ourselves what we want and never share our true desires. A man cannot fulfill you if he doesn't know how you can be fulfilled! He cannot help make your dreams come true if he doesn't know what they are. He cannot knock your socks off in bed unless you show him the way. Though the naysayer will insist you can't teach an old dog new tricks, the fact is, every guy is a work in progress, a diamond in the rough, a raw hunk of marble waiting to be chiseled. You, my lovelies, can take the lead with pleasure. You will be surprised at how willing your partner will be, once you let that guy in on your world of desires.

Guys tend to get kind of crusty and dusty when they have no women around them. You all know those old bachelors—they are like something from Grandma's attic, covered with crust and dust. If the guy has been in direct contact with a woman—if he has been helping her fulfill her desires, either sensually or otherwise—some of her life force is bound to rub off on him. It takes some Goddess juice to polish up a guy so he looks civilized enough for a woman to be interested in him. You know that expression, "All the best ones are married"? The reason married guys look so good is that they have a woman's influence—all over them. Naturally they look more attractive than Mr. Single who hasn't had a date in months. The ones that haven't had women in a while need more polishing.

Women polish *themselves* up with their own enthusiasm. The Goddesses who come to class saying things like, "There are so many amazing guys out there. I am having so much fun being single, so much fun with dating!"—these gals won't be single for long if they don't want to be. Men are drawn helplessly toward a woman who is enjoying herself. The reason men find a happy woman intoxicating is that on some level, every guy knows that a woman who can enjoy herself solo will be more than able to enjoy him. Men can be perceptive that way. Men have a very important undervalued trait—they respond to women.

Now, I happen to love the story of Beauty and the Beast. It is one Disney classic I am proud to own and enjoy watching with my daughter. Why? 'Cause it reveals the truth between men and women. When a woman approves of and appreciates a beasty guy, he transforms into a prince. Is Mama saying that every man is a beast? Well, yes—every man starts out ignorant and uninformed about the world of woman.

The secret is that men really want to contribute to our happiness. Go ahead, read that sentence again. You got it right. Men want to join the crusade for an ecstatic you. They simply don't know how. Engaging these willing partners simply requires a shift in your approach. I'm telling you, calm that itchy trigger finger. You have to stop attacking them and learn to recruit guys to your cause instead. Once you start sharing your desires with men, you'll see that not only are you on your way to creating an unprecedented partnership, but the guy is thrilled to be along for the ride.

When I teach my "Mama Gena Gives It Up to Men" class, I am overwhelmed, moved, and profoundly touched by the guys' willingness and interest in what makes us women tick. They want to know everything—what makes us happy, how we like to be kissed and touched, what we want. Ah, that's the ticket—what we want. This is the greatest mystery to men—what do women want? It is also the greatest mystery to most women.

I think that this is the biggest shock to my Goddesses—that men do not come finished. We all think we're looking for this super soul mate who understands us, reads our minds, and knows how to fulfill us. We have been duped by that myth of the white knight, the prince, the rescuer who will take us away from our unfulfilled life to a magic kingdom of happiness. In these stories he knows the way, he casts aside all obstacles, and he needs no help from his delicate damsel. Well, my darlings, the faster you can banish that silly legend from your minds, the better. Anyone who has ever been to the Magic Kingdom knows there ain't no magic there—it's nothing but long lines, boring rides, bad food, and overpriced souvenirs.

Create a new story in which you ride that powerful white steed into the happily-ever-after yourself. If it suits you, maybe you can swing a stud muffin onto the back of your saddle as you head for the sunset, but you, my dears, have the reins, you're driving this vision—and all you really need to fulfill it is you! Life is not a waiting game. Here are a few basic principles that might help you follow your own yellow brick road:

Treasure Yourself

If you want to be treasured, you have to treasure yourself first and then show someone how to treasure you. This is going to be a challenge. Many of us gals have not done the research necessary—on ourselves—to begin to give guys the information they need to make us happy. After all, if we don't know what we want, how can we tell them? But not only do we not take the time to investigate our desires, we expect guys to show up with all the facts about making us happy. This assumption is as irresponsible as putting an investment banker in charge of a vegetable farm. He may like eating carrots but he sure won't know when to plow, when to sow, and when to reap. Mr.

Banker Man may be perfectly willing, and interested enough, to learn all those things—but he, like you, has a lot to learn before he'll be ready to run that farm.

You want him to give you a massage? Pick up the dry cleaning? Go clothes shopping with you? Loosen your lips! Ask him. Asking nicely is a good first step. Speak. Anything is better than a cold silence filled with the expectation that he will read your mind. Even if you date a psychic, there will still be important areas he won't be able to pick up on. It's up to you, Goddesses—you have to discover your desires and then utter them. You can't have it all if you don't ask for it.

Stop Trying to Be the Good Girlfriend (or Wife)

Many women who come to me are obsessed about figuring out what men want. These women are barking up the wrong tree. Your success in romance has nothing to do with your attention to your particular guy. If a woman is spending her time with a man trying to serve him as a way of keeping him, that guy will go away, and fast!

He will go away even if the woman serving him is good-looking and wealthy. I had a gorgeous Sister Goddess from a fabulously wealthy family in Venezuela. Daniela was thirty and not married, much to her and her family's disappointment. Now, our culture is chauvinistic, but Latin culture is *mucho macho* chauvinistic. This gal was trained to look pretty, be polite, say the right things—basically she was taught to act like a hood ornament. When she would date a guy, Daniela would never expose herself. All of her and her date's activities focused on what he wanted to do. Daniela was deeply committed to her zombiehood—so much so that she would enter into internal hysteria and chaos at just the thought of telling a man the truth. He would say, "Where would you like to go for dinner?" She would say, "Wherever you want to go." He would ask if he could kiss her good night. Daniela would say, "If you want to." If a guy did something to offend her, Daniela would never let him know. Her dates never knew if they were winning Daniela's affections or losing them, so after a date or two, they would go away.

Daniela's behavior was so ingrained that even Mama Gena couldn't convince her to give up her subservience and go for pleasure. Needless to say, Daniela dropped out of Mama Gena's class. And just like the guys she dated, I have no idea why. She never said. She was polite and well bred and cooperative, but she never voiced an opinion or a desire. She simply moved back to Venezuela, back to her parents' house, back to her solitary life.

Attracting a man obviously has nothing to do with prettiness or charm or sexiness, with being thin, or with having big breasts, lots of money, an exotic look, foreign accent, or anything else. Being attractive to men depends on whether you approve of yourself, you can express your desires and enjoy your desires in a man's presence. You have to be confident enough to positively flaunt what pleases you. It's intoxicating to see a woman enjoying what she wants, and the presence of such a fulfilled woman is irresistible to a man.

Remember, a man loves to see a woman enjoying herself, and he loves to be able to add to that enjoyment. But a man also knows, on some level, that he can't possibly handle complete responsibility for a woman's fulfillment. A shy woman who won't fess up to her desires will never get a guy, whereas a shy woman who quietly exposes her desires can hook any guy in her path. Think about this, my lovelies. If you doubt it, take a look at another common dynamic that happens between women and men.

Stop Being Desperate

I should know, I've lived this story. When I first met my husband, it had been a long time since I had had a guy in my life. I was all over him. One of his teachers told Bruce that when he came to see me, he should throw a huge hunk of meat in my cage before he went in for a visit. I mean, I was a wild and hungry gal! What I learned from my behavior back then is that a woman has to handle her horniness. Horny is not attractive. When a guy sees a horny woman, he feels like, "Yikes! She's insatiable! There is no way I could ever gratify her!"

Horniness is not permanent. It is temporary if a woman is willing to pleasure herself, give herself attention, and get attention from other sources besides the guy she hopes to land. A man can pleasure a sated woman because she doesn't need him, she is already happy. He can be the icing on her cake. It's way too much pressure to be the icing, the cake, and the baker all at once, which is what happens when a woman places the responsibility for her happiness solely in the hands of a man.

A gal who sees *POTENTIAL HUSBAND* tattooed across the forehead of every man she meets is certainly not paying attention to her desires, and she's not even paying attention to the men who come into her life. She's taking a little head trip and driving slowly. It's interesting—often a marriage-obsessed woman will come to me for coaching and she will say, "I want a husband, but there are just no good guys out there." I know immediately she is going to need some emergency Mama Gena rehabilitation. Before she does anything else, she's got to notice there are millions of wonderful men out there. If she's willing to commit herself totally to having fun wherever she is, with whomever's already at hand, she won't have to find the one. He'll find her.

So a woman who wants to find a husband can just put that goal on the back burner and start enjoying the men in her life, sharing with the guys she comes across and telling them what she truly wants. If a woman does get into marriage with no training in enjoying men beforehand, she's committed herself to the equivalent of the relationship marathon before ever having trained a mile.

Put the Bitch Back in Her Cage Where She Belongs

When you start getting that self-righteous feeling in a relationship, that's the kiss of death. "He should do this because I did that," "He better, or else," "I deserve *this*"—these are all signals that lead straight to being right and also being very, very alone. (None of us have any rights, really. We have opportunities and privileges, not rights.) It is at this moment and others like it that every S.G. has to make a choice—pleasure or anger. This is a crossroads that you will hit many times over in a relationship: Shall I choose pleasure, or anger? Now, one of the most fantastic pieces of coaching I ever received was how to tone down my screech. I never realized the degree of anger and impatience that crept into my voice when I talked to men until I was made aware of it.

My screech modulation began when I was thirty-three years old just after I met Bruce. Poor Bruce was on the receiving end of my thirty-three years of disappointment, anger, and frustration with men, which I ("Who, me?") didn't even know I had. Thanks to my friend, J.B., I was on "tone patrol" and softened the harsh edge in my voice before it ruined my relationship with Bruce. When I asked Bruce for something or told him something, I spoke as a friend, not an enemy.

At least this was the case when I remembered to be on tone patrol, which wasn't all the time. Bruce became my buddy in my tone patrol—when tensions rose he'd help me find a friendlier way of communicating. It helps that he has a great sense of humor. He would say things like, "I'd sure love to do that for you, but could you ask me nicer?"

These days, when women hate the spot they are in they feel victimized, and, their knee-jerk reaction is to lash out at the man who put them there. But no man put us in our spot—we are all products of our time, our conditioning, our circumstance. We are all in this together. Men may be ignorant about women, but their mothers and sisters and girlfriends and wives kept them that way. We can do better. We can begin to reveal the truth to each other—nicely. We can share our perspective with men in a friendly manner that benefits both parties. This can be a riveting challenge for an angry bitch. But once she embraces a kinder, gentler approach, she will feel her anger melt away and her fulfillment grow. Isn't that a good trade-off?

Practice Defensive Dating

When S.G. Charlotte came to her first class with Mama, she could hardly name one little desire she had. Now she is well on her way to knowing a great deal about what she likes, and therefore closer to finding a guy. She had discovered she liked going to restaurants by herself, taking the time to call her friends, organizing intimate cocktail parties. During the third week of class Charlotte asked if it was ever OK to call a guy. "Of course," I said. "Yes, yes, absolutely yes!" (This is my answer if you're bubbling over with fun and desire. Then, it's fabulous to call. It's probably not the greatest idea in the world if you are calling out of desperation, simply because guys can smell desperation and they don't react well to it!) So, S.G. Charlotte called a guy. They went out on a date. She didn't have that much fun, but she was proud of herself for venturing beyond her old boundaries. The next week, Charlotte went to a picnic and flirted with some guys she didn't know. She asked one of them to walk her home. He did, and he asked for her number. They went out, and this guy Charlotte *really* likes.

But Charlotte is also practicing what Mama calls "defensive dating." She's dating a bunch of guys at once, having a good time all around without putting all her eggs into one little basket. Even when she meets what she considers to be the right guy, it's good for a woman, like Charlotte, to continue to date a number of men because it keeps her spirits up. When you date a husband candidate, his responses to you can become unnaturally important. If you are getting along great, you feel great. But if you are going through a difficult period, it is good to have another guy to remind you that you are gorgeous, attractive, and wonderful. Allowing your opinion of yourself to depend on one guy's approval of you is not good for anyone. Defensive dating keeps you aware of your best qualities at all times.

Don't Throw in the Towel So Quickly

One of the great road blocks in the man/woman highway is women's tendency to give up before they start to drive. If we meet a guy and he's not rich enough, we write him off. If we meet a guy and he doesn't know how to kiss, we banish him.

Many women cry defeat when faced with the smallest challenge to their desires. This is what S.G. Claudine did, and it cost her the big love of her life. S.G. Claudine was dating Ralph, from Detroit. She felt he was "the one" and happily told everyone so—until one day when another woman came along. Ralph took her out a few times, just checking out new territory. When S.G. Claudine heard he was dating someone else, she bailed out of the relationship. Without even telling her guy why she was leaving him, S.G. Claudine broke up with Ralph. What happened was that Claudine decided, all by herself, that Ralph would probably prefer the other woman over her. S.G. Claudine's insecurity about what she had to offer Ralph and the world in general came between her and her dreams.

Claudine felt vindicated when Ralph dated and then went on to marry the other woman. But what else was he going to do? S.G. Claudine bailed out before the games even began. Ralph never had the chance to choose her over the other woman. There's another way to look at this whole scenario—Ralph could have married the other woman on the rebound from Claudine. But given the way she forfeited her position in Ralph's life, Claudine will never know what the real story was. No guts, no glory. It takes a woman with the courage of her convictions to have her way in the man/woman game.

Case in point. There was this perfectly adorable, recently divorced guy, Bernie, knocking around my Sister Goddesses. For a long while, no one grabbed him. He was a bit battered from his divorce and none of my beauties could see the prince underneath the frog. All Bernie needed was a kiss to blossom into his full handsomeness, but no one really wanted to get slime on their lips, until S.G. Amy came along.

When S.G. Amy went out with Bernie, she left the date thinking, "Yikes! I just met the man I am going to marry!" But what Bernie was thinking was, "Nice girl. Too bad nothing will ever come of this relationship."

After all, Bernie was just extricating himself from a nasty divorce and could not even conceive of a relationship going well. He had never been in a good relationship—in fact, he had never even seen one!

Amy sure had her work cut out for her. But blossoming Goddess that she was, Amy rose to the challenge. One of the noblest aspects of S.G. Amy was her willingness to invest in Bernie for the long term, and to celebrate small victories with him along the way. She wanted a husband, she wanted a family, so Amy did what it took to bring Bernie along into her fantasy. Bernie was resisting the idea of dating her exclusively, so Amy figured, since she was still single, she might as well date other guys. This was a great idea. Not only did it help remind Amy how attractive and fun she was, but she realized, after talking to her dates, that she had been putting way too much pressure on Bernie and it was time to lighten up. The bonus was, Amy's dating other men made Bernie jealous. Bernie realized that he loved Amy in his life and didn't want to risk losing her. So Amy eased up on her pressure on Bernie, and he responded more favorably to her input.

They had so much fun together that after a few months Amy thought it might be good to check out living together, as a first step. When Amy mentioned this to Bernie, he screamed "No!" But Amy was clever enough remember the Mama Gena axiom "Pay less attention to what a guy says than to where his feet are." Amy noticed that while Bernie squawked at the idea of any kind of commitment, he slept over at her apartment nearly every night. After a year of their bedroom slippers living side by side, Amy decided to start charging Bernie rent. It was then that Bernie suggested that maybe they should look at buying a place together. Amy was ecstatic. She celebrated. She rejoiced. She was making headway!

And Amy was right. Two years later, Bernie and Amy were married. The most important thing in this little tale, my lovelies, is that S.G. Amy saw Bernie as her man. That's the key to her amazingly good results. If this savvy S.G. had not been so secure in her desires, her man's resistance would have been fatal to the relationship. Instead, Amy kept hold of her dreams with both hands and was rewarded.

Enjoy a Little Resistance

OK, OK, you may say, why bother with our desires when the resistance is so strong? I say that resistance actually makes the game more fun. Obstacles give color and flavor to the game. You can't imagine the hilarity and joy at S.G. Amy and Bernie's wedding. Or the fun they have reminiscing about their courtship, as they bounce their baby on their knees. Resistance is the stuff that great novels, poetry, and love stories that live through centuries are made of. As women, we want to be heroines in our own romance novels and subsist on nothing but the glory and power of love and passion. Ulysses and Penelope, Elinor Dashwood and Edward Ferrars from Jane Austen's *Sense and Sensibility,* Prince Vlad and Mina from Bram Stoker's *Dracula*—it is all so worth waking up for.

Women often ask me if their guy is just too resistant to be worked with. I don't think that's possible. I think any degree of resistance can be acceptable, as long as it's fun for you. If you date a guy who says *no* too much for your liking, fine—pass on him. Find a guy who says *yes* more easily. It does not mean your *no* man is impossible to get—all it means is you want one with less resistance. There are millions of men out there. There is a lid for every pot, as my grandmother would say. Go get yourself a fella who is fun for you. The key is fun. People think the key is love or commitment. That is not the case. You love the people you have fun with. A man you are having fun with will love you forever. Commitment doesn't lead to fun. Love doesn't lead to fun. People sometimes do very violent, hurtful things in the name of love or commitment. But fun always leads to love.

Show Him Approval

I am sure you know women who are amazingly demanding bitches in the presence of their husbands. In these cases everyone always asks the same question: "Why is he still with her?" To me it's obvious why men stay with a demanding shrew. This woman is making good use of her husband—she is spending his money, having his kids, and giving him some direction. She is going after what she wants and is appreciating him just enough to keep him. Now, Mama is not recommending that you keep your man on this demand-only diet—it never leads to happiness. But as options go, I would say being a demanding bitch is an improvement over keeping your mouth shut and never letting your man hear what you want.

Better still would be enjoying and appreciating that special person in your life. A guy requires a certain amount of approval to stay in a relationship. When your demands on him outweigh your approval of him, your man will eventually go away.

Now, let's take a closer look at what Mama means by approval. When I first bring it up in my classes, many Sister Goddesses want to know just what passes for approval when it comes to their men. They want to show it. I tell them, and I will tell you, that approving of your man is as simple as the way you say, "Yum yum," when he hands you a piece of your favorite chocolate cake. Or the way you smile when you see him across a crowded room at a bar. Or when you first meet him and he sees you thinking, "Oooh la la," or simply, "Nice." It boils down to enjoying your life in his presence. That is the tricky part—the enjoying part. Most of the women who cross my path are operating on a deficit—they are chronically underattentioned, underpleasured, undersexed, underfulfilled. When a woman on a starvation diet first sees a guy who looks halfway decent, she hurls herself at him the way a drowning person hurls herself at a lifeguard. Her desperation threatens to drown them both.

Steer Him in the Right Direction

Guys require a lot of direction, but the upside of the work we put in is amazing. Men will move forward with enthusiasm, in any direction we point them. For example, if you go out to a restaurant together and love it, a man most likely will want to go there every night. You may want to go there once, and try a new restaurant the next time and the time after that. This is the moment to tell your guy how wonderful that restaurant was and how much you would love a new experience. You don't have to limit yourself because a man is different from you, nor do you have to give in to his vision. Stick to your own desires and gently steer your man onto your path.

Years ago, my husband took me out to an Italian restaurant and we ordered tiramisù for dessert. I loved it so much that I gushed over it. As a result, my husband brought me home another one of these delicious desserts the very next day, from an Italian bakery. Two days later, he stopped at another Italian restaurant and picked up a new tiramisù. And so on and so on, until I had a refrigerator full of tiramisù. At first I was so appreciative. Then I wanted to stop him, but I didn't know how to do so without hurting his feelings. Finally, when there were five of them in the refrigerator, I was overwhelmed by his enthusiasm, and actually annoyed by it. I screamed, "Stop with the tiramisù!" When the dust settled, I told Bruce that I loved sweets but I wanted their pleasure only occasionally. I suggested that if he wanted to get me something consistently, flowers would be nice. Flowers die, so new ones are always appreciated. Telling the truth, nicely, one step at a time, is the way to get your way in the man/woman game.

I suppose you noticed that I didn't do that. I just yelled at my sweetie. So, sometimes we miss a few. It happens. But the wonderful thing about the man/woman game is how forgiving it is. It is the most intense game on this planet. It brings out the best in us, the worst in us, and everything in between. And there is also room in it for almost any kind of mistake, as long as there is fun present. Now, men do not stay with women because of *commitment.* Look at the divorce rate. When it ceases to be fun, they go. Actually, it's often pretty hard to get rid of men, even then because we can be pretty fun even when we are screaming at them. A few days of fun, at the beginning, can get you through a few years with a guy. Look at Liz Taylor and Richard Burton—he actually married her *twice.* He knew what he was getting into, but that fun they had must have been really something.

Bruce and I now laugh about the tiramisù thing. I was able to eat one again only about ten years later. And he does bring me flowers—every week. I am still working on my communication style, finding ways to tell him more intimate truths in a friendly fashion. Men and women are really alien to each other, and the union of aliens is delicate business. Partnership is always an experiment, a work in progress. But one thing we women should focus more on is how we can positively reinforce our messages to the special guys in our lives. Men are so grateful and responsive when we make the effort to communicate our desires to them, even when it doesn't look that way at first glance.

Employ the Training Cycle

What does Mama mean when she slings around the word "training"? Webster says: "train: to direct the growth of, to form by instruction, to teach so as to make fit, qualified or proficient." In other words, deliver information to your partner that will make him indispensable to you. You may be wondering: Is this fair use of the guy? Absolutely. A woman isn't just taking when she trains, she is giving, too.

Over the years, this system has helped me a lot. The training cycle is a three-part communication cycle that allows you to get your way, nicely. It breaks the truth down into consumable bites. Sometimes you have a list of four thousand ways you want your partner to improve. This is fine, but you want to give him one at a time. He can't process four thousand at once. It pays for you to be patient. The training cycle helps you stay focused on the one issue you'd like to improve at the moment, and to focus on it in a friendly manner. (And by the way, this training cycle works on anyone—man, woman, child, employer.) This is how it works:

1. Show your partner he is right.

2. Give him a problem he can solve.

3. Acknowledge him.

So, if this was me and my tiramisù escapade, it would go something like this:

1. Bruce, you are so sweet and I want to thank you so much for the tiramisù.

2. Could you bring me flowers next time?

3. Thank you.

This sounds a little—how shall I say? Contrived? Well, why not? I've heard so many stories of problem-solving attempts gone awry. Why not try a method that provides your man with approval and satisfaction, and makes way for you to satisfy any new desire? Just try this. See where it gets you and your man. You may be surprised at how much you end up using it.

Once you begin airing your desires to your man nicely, you are on the right track. Then all you have to do is—practice, practice, practice. That is all it takes, really, to become a wonderful man trainer. Practice paying attention to your pleasure, your desires, and then finding ways to communicate every detail of your truth to your man, nicely. He wants to know you, not a made-up, fake version of you. Give him all of you and you will never want to be apart from him. And he'll feel the same. You'll be amazed how this simple technique will serve your needs as well as his. This technique has brought my husband and me much closer. Bruce is my closest, best friend. I miss him when we are apart, and I can't wait to share every detail of my day with him. Be patient, keep sharing your desires. The closeness that results is worth the wait. It took Bruce and me twelve years to get this close.

While you're looking for your "right one," just train the one you're with. Train your brother, train your sons, train your boss, train your guy friends. March down the training highway. The worst thing that can happen is you will leave a bunch of guys better off than you found them. They will have learned some truth about women. And men are starved for truth about women. While you may think or feel that you are training only these guys, in truth you are also training yourself. The best outcome of your efforts will be your discovery of what *you* love.

Exercise 1: A Quiz on Owning and Operating Your Men

Determine the level of your training skills and readiness with this survey:

1. How man-friendly is your life?

   A. Do you have more than one towel in your bathroom?

   B. Is there room in your closet?

   C. Do you have two nightstands by your bed?

   D. Is your bed a double or bigger?

If you answered *no* any of these questions, be willing to make some changes. If you build it, he will come.

2. How do you respond to a man's resistance? When he doesn't call you within forty-eight hours after a date

   A. You write him off and yell, "Next!"

   B. You call him and tell him what a great time you had.

   C. You happily await his call while you entertain yourself with other men and are genuinely excited when he finally calls.

If you chose A, you are letting the man run the show and not taking responsibility for your good time. If you chose B, there is hope for you. And you get extra credit if you picked C.

3. *When a man says no to your request, you*

A. Yell at him and get it for yourself.

B. You stop wanting it and forget about it.

C. You see how you could have more fun seducing him into your great idea.

If you chose A or B you are not using a guy for his maximum potential. If you give up that easily, you will never get what you want. Be willing to ask more than once. If you chose C you are already an advanced man trainer.

4. *The best way to make your guy happy is*

A. Do whatever he wants.

B. Praise him for all the great things he does for you.

C. Enjoy your life and get everything you want.

A may seem like the obvious answer, but actually, men live to serve women. He will lose interest in you if you don't use him for your pleasure. B is a good start, but you can't stop there. The most attractive thing a woman can do for a man is to give him a way to serve her. So think of things you want and tell him. If you chose C, you are probably already married or you have many boyfriends, and they are all crazy about you.

Exercise 2: The Training Cycle

The training cycle is a communication process that enables us to get what we want, nicely, from anyone. Most women have a knee-jerk response to say *no* when someone, especially a man, makes us an offer. We would rather do it ourselves! One of the nicest things we can do for a man is to permit him to serve us. Say *yes* every time a man offers to do something for you. Coach your man to do something for you in exactly the way you'd like it done.

The Training Cycle

1. Show your partner he is right.
2. Give him a problem he can solve.
3. Acknowledge him.

Exercise 3: Learning from the Pros

Check out a number of fabulous man-training movies. Films like *Hobson's Choice* and *The African Queen* allow you to see true S.G.'s in man-training action.

In *Hobson's Choice,* notice how Maggie leads Will down the path to her goals, step by step, without being stopped by his resistances. Do you see how she actually enjoys the game of how he resists her? See how you can apply Maggie's techniques to your own life. *The African*

Queen shows how a woman's vision drives a man to the status of a hero, when he supports her goals. This journey also leads to a great romance—who could want anything more than a hero and a lover all rolled into one fabulous package!

❋ ❋ ❋

The object here is to have your way with the men in your life—it's the nicest thing you can do for them. Do you want to experiment further with the vast power of your desire and its impact on the world? Good—because that's where we are heading next.

Lesson 9

The Womanly Art of Inviting Abundance

I now release the gold-mine within me. I am linked with an endless golden stream of prosperity which comes to me under grace and in perfect ways.

—Florence Scovel Shinn, *The Game of Life and How to Play It*

If you are like most new Womanly Arts students, you don't have any idea about your potential for prosperity. Your pickin's in life could be so good—so bountiful that at first you won't be able to absorb the tremendousness of your ability to create! The days of "a room of one's own" have expanded to a home of one's own, a business of one's own, even an entire industry of one's own. Just take a look at the fabulous Miss Martha Stewart—she has created an empire out of the domestic Goddess. Or the incredible Oprah—turning her curiosity into a corporate industry. And my beloved Madonna—the icon of our millennium. These gals stood on their own two feet, took the world by storm, and made an impact on all of us. Each of them started from scratch—and has realized her own vision of success on her own terms.

What we can take away from their examples is that this level of achievement, this individual path to greatness, is an option available for any of us with the same kind of drive, the same sense of mission.

You are now familiar with the art of flirting, of falling in love with yourself, of communicating with the opposite sex. You recognize the phenomenal impact of your desires. In this lesson I want to show you the art of harnessing this force of nature that is you, and using it to attract life's riches. Most people think you attain things or accomplish goals purely through hard work. Work is certainly one way to get what you want, but it's only one way. We women can conjure anything we want simply by wanting, and by enjoying the experience of savoring our desires. You have heard the phrase "If you build it, they will come." Women play on a different playing field. Our refrain could be: "If you want it and enjoy the wanting, it will come even quicker, and with more fun, than if you built it." And if you feel like doing some building, that's cool, too.

Check out a wonderful book called *The Game of Life and How to Play It,* written by Florence Scovel Shinn in the 1920s. Shinn was a metaphysician, a Christian Scientist, and a spiritual teacher who believed in the transformational power of thought, and in our limitless potential as human beings. I have all my Goddesses read this book because her ideas appeal to women of every faith, and you can tuck this slim little volume in your purse and remind yourself of your limitlessness throughout the day.

Her most compelling idea is, you can win the game of life simply by thinking you will. It's like Creative Visualization—if in your mind's eye you can see yourself getting what you want, that vision has the power to make it so. It's all a game. If you play the game of working hard for a living and denying yourself things, that will be a self-fulfilling prophecy. You will be enslaved to your own viewpoint. If you play the game of "I am a genius artist and I will make a fortune through doing what I love," you will create that for yourself. S.G. Alma did just that. Although she is a famous rock singer, Alma never went to music school. She never took a voice lesson. One of her ex-boyfriends was a rock legend who gave her access to the top people in the music industry. The following year she had her first performance in New York. Alma simply envisioned herself as a rock star. She had only been around successful singers, so in her experience good musicians became successful very easily and simply. And so she became successful. Doubt never entered her mind—she just went for what made her happy and found success along the way.

Your dreams are not too big for you, you would not have them if they were not just the right size and shape for the individual you are. They are blueprints of your future fulfillment. Everything you want, you can have. Don't worry about money—the price tag will get in your way only if you let it. If you could trust your dreams half as much as you doubt them, you would get everything you want. Florence Scovel Shinn says, "Every desire, uttered or unexpressed, is a demand. We are often startled by having a wish suddenly fulfilled."

Sometimes we are naturally good at having certain things. For example, I am very good at real estate. I have an uncanny ability to stumble across exactly the right apartment at exactly the right time. S.G. Justine is great at coming across free designer clothes, and strangely enough, her friends have developed the knack as well. As you saw in Lesson 2, S.G. Margaret got the knack of hotel upgrades after being with S.G. Daphne. So one way to increase your powers of attraction is to be around other women who can conjure more than you have imagined possible for yourself.

The manifestation of desire is what I call "conjuring." Conjurings never require money. They are living tributes to our power as women to attract.

One excellent conjurer I know is S.G. Bess, who drove in from New Jersey to take one of my Womanly Arts courses. Bess was nervous to drive all the way into the city because she was afraid she wouldn't find a parking spot. In fact, the parking issue almost kept her from taking the class. The first night, Bess overcame her doubts about the parking dilemma and drove in to Manhattan. She pulled up in front of my brownstone, and there, right in front, was a big empty parking spot. Not only did S.G. Bess not have to pay for parking but she felt she had received a sign that she was in the right place at the right time. This Goddess class was where she was supposed to be.

That first conjuring was spontaneous, but interestingly enough, Bess was able to park in this same spot week after week. Bess enjoyed thinking about the parking spot so much that she conjured it for six weeks straight. Other women in the class had to pull their cars into nearby parking lots time and again because space is so hard to find. But S.G. Bess got so good at conjuring, she became the precourse entertainment for other Goddesses. Bess's classmates would wait on the stoop, just to see her get her spot every week.

Conjuring something requires the expectation of pure pleasure. You have to salivate the way you do when you are hungry for a lobster roll with shoestring fries, or devil's food cake, or fried clams. You don't worry too much about whether or not you get the clams or lobster roll or cake—you just enjoy the thought of them. When you savor a desire like that, and give it time to really come to life in your mind and imagination, you actually make things happen. The beauty of conjuring is that you can bring anything your way. Yes, anything.

S.G. Meryl quit her bone-crushing job as a designer in New York City's garment district to paint vulva paintings. Meryl had been an artist her whole life. She loved painting nudes, especially female nudes. She had become a designer because everyone told her she couldn't make a living as an artist, but she had always wanted to give it a try. I, on the other hand, had always wanted a vulva painting in my vestibule. (We found out, after the vestibule was painted, that vulvas were a common design in the paleolithic era. They were painted at the openings of caves to signify a holy space. This added to our fun.) So Meryl painted a giant vulva mural in the entry to my home. This so inspired her that she decided to quit her job and make a career of the feminine form on canvas. S.G. Meryl had no idea if she could make a living doing such an odd thing, but that didn't stop her. The day she quit her job, Meryl was offered part-time work at double the pay by another company that wanted her skills as a designer. She accepted the position gladly as a way of making her transition.

A few months later, Meryl's friend introduced her to someone at a huge clothing manufacturing company. This place is known for their men's T-shirts and boxer shorts. She gave a presentation about her hand-painted T-shirts and panties, and everyone was so swept away by her enthusiasm that they are going to manufacture and publicize her products for her. Talk about conjuring!

Actually, our ability to conjure can be very scary. S.G. Meryl was so overwhelmed by this manifestation of her power that she tucked the project in a drawer and did not do a thing that they asked her to do. All they wanted was for her to design the tags and labels for the product. She was so blown away by her own power to conjure and the warm reception to her desires in the world that she froze for a few months. Mama had to snap her out of it, and now she is finished with her work and awaiting free manufacturing and free publicity. Her dream has hurtled itself into her lap.

The trip to your dreams is not an easy one. Sometimes you may miss a meal or two, or a credit card payment or a rent deadline. But there are people who don't follow their dreams who face those same situations as well. I have never known anyone who followed their deepest desires with all-out enthusiasm and failed. It is almost as if the universe gives you a leg up, or a helping hand, when you really go for what your heart desires.

Another way to hone your ability to attract life's bounty is to pleasure and treasure yourself. If you can't give yourself flowers, it is going to be nearly impossible for you to receive flowers from anyone else. If you don't give yourself orgasms, it is going to be really difficult for you to receive one from someone else. Treasure yourself in every area that you wish to be treasured, and you will increase your ability to have what you want and to enjoy your life.

Another great way to attract abundance is to give it to others. Begin by doing small anonymous acts of good. Elect yourself the good fairy. Clean up a public rest room for the next person. Pick up a Coke can that someone else left on the street and throw it in a trash pail. Send flowers anonymously to someone you know is having a tough day. Leave a box of chocolates on a coworker's desk. You get the idea—small acts that make other people's lives better will expand your ability to receive goodies from others and from the world. You end up feeling better about yourself. You feel more deserving because you made an investment in the good. So when the universe opens a door for you, you are ready to say "Yes!"

These little habits, when added to your routine, will increase your ability to conjure more and more, which releases you from your bondage to money. Money is simply the slave driver we all serve until we break free, and allow ourselves to surrender to our pleasure. Life is much more fulfilling and exciting when you surrender to your dreams rather than enslave yourself to money. Our desires lead us to all the money we could ever require. We may still feel envious of what other women have, but all that feeling envious means is that you have pinpointed a new desire. You would not feel this way if it weren't your desire—something that *you* want. The spot where women go wrong is when they think, "Oh, if she's having *that,* then I certainly can't have it." How about, "If she is having that, and it looks good to me, then I am next in line"? Embrace your envy. Love it, pay attention to it. If you do, the desires beneath it will be unearthed with tremendous speed. There is enough of everything in this world for everyone to have what they want, and more.

Now, S.G. Natalie wanted diamonds. She wanted diamonds so much that she could barely stand it when other women wore them. One day in class, S.G. Justine came in with a beautiful diamond band that her ex-boyfriend had given her. Justine was so good with having guys give her stuff that she was even able to have the ring after she had broken up with the guy. S.G. Natalie said she was totally jealous of this and that she, too, wanted diamonds. It was the first time she had felt good enough about herself and her desire to admit it to anyone. Two weeks later, Natalie's grandmother gave her a beautiful multidiamond ring that had belonged to her mother. The grandmother could have given it to Natalie's sister, or Natalie's mom, but she gave it to Natalie. It wasn't until Natalie admitted her jealousy and admitted her desire that she was able to conjure her grandma's giving her the diamond ring.

I grew up with the legend of my mother, Bebe, who at age two was completely connected to her true wishes. The story goes that during the depths of the Depression Bebe went walking on the boardwalk of Atlantic City with her big sister Gertie. She stopped in front of a toy store. There was a beautifully dressed doll in the window, which probably cost the equivalent of a month's wages for my grandfather. But a two-year-old gives not a fig for any value higher than her own desire. Bebe sobbed relentlessly for the doll, unwilling to leave the store, unwilling to move on without it. As Gertie tried to drag her away, Bebe screamed louder. Finally a tall, well-dressed man appeared and asked Gertie why Bebe was crying. Gertie told him that her sister wanted the doll in the window. He went into the store and bought the doll for her, then disappeared.

Now, what was the dynamic at work here? I say: Call elicits response. Appetite conjures production. When a woman wants, there is always a way for her to get whatever her heart desires. Money is no object, neither is time or distance. Appetite can move mountains in microseconds. Fulfilling our hearts' desires is an eternally enchanting game and one that we will always win when we play!

Does it sound as if Mama is grooming a greedy gang of gals? I hope so. True abundance and generosity can come only from a woman who has *hers.* Having confidence in one's desires comes from having them fulfilled and noticing the consequences of operating from a full tank of gas, rather than an empty one. Sister Goddess Marla arrived in class a shy, almost girlish young woman. She had just broken up with her boyfriend, and her father, whom she adored, was ill with a rare form of leukemia. S.G. Marla was not really in the mood to have fun or trust her desires, but she had put herself in the class because she figured that mourning had brought her only so far and she had farther she wanted to go. She indulged in the pampering exercises, bought herself some sexy new clothes, and began to date again. What she found was, she became more confident. She began to trust herself. She began to realize her desires had value and impact on the world.

As she thought about her father's health and the way his doctors were treating him, she realized she was uneasy with his care. She had never been effective at talking her father into anything, so she was a bit nervous to ask him to listen to her idea for a change in his treatment. But with her newfound courage she made an appointment to talk with a new doctor for herself, and invited her dad to come if he wanted to. He not only met this new doctor, but he ended up switching to his care. This new doctor started him on a program that ended up saving his life. He is now cancer free. This happened because S.G. Marla was selfish about having her way, for the first time in her life. Women's desires always lead to something wonderful.

That they can create abundance is a phenomenon that tickles my S.G.'s to no end. These gals come from all backgrounds, all socioeconomic brackets, but all of them can afford a cup of coffee anytime they want. Yet when I have them practice their Bitte et Chat, or flirtation, they come back to class delighted by how their flirtation led to some deli guy giving them a free coffee, or a maître d' buying them a drink or dessert, or a parking attendant squeezing them in after the lot was full. The raw fun of desire let loose creates more levity, more power, and more overall hilarity among my S.G.'s than an outfit bought at Chanel or a ski weekend.

Everything I have attracted by desire has meant significantly more to me than anything that came strictly through an outlay of cash.

I once conjured a mink coat. This is how it happened. I went to Bergdorf's with my friend Melissa. We tried on mink coats. We had such a good time and I found myself to be so stunning in that luxurious pelt that I brought my husband back a few weeks later and tried on all the furs for him. The saleslady explained to us that minks were not very nice animals—they had the personalities of mean rats, she said, so it was justified to make coats out of them. I hated that statement, yet I still lusted for fur. I couldn't help myself. I had a desire for mink that just wouldn't die. What happened? This year, S.G. Ali showed up at class one day with a large bag. Inside was an enormous, gorgeous, floor-length mink. S.G. Ali said she'd had enough of it and wanted Mama G. and the rest of the class to have it. A couple of years before, S.G. Ali had bought herself the coat to cheer herself up when she was blue. She no longer needed it. That's how appetite works. The universe grants our desire when we put it out there.

It was interesting—I had lost my appetite for buying a new fur because of the animal-rights issue, but to receive a fur that had already been purchased seemed different. It seemed that I would honor the animals by using it, instead of letting it go to waste. It was also really fun to have a house mink that all the S.G.'s could use as they needed. That coat went out on a lot of glam evenings—one gal wore it on a date for the opera, another donned it for a special formal party, other S.G.'s simply wanted to wear fur for a few weeks, so they borrowed the coat.

You know what's funny about the mink? I never wore it once. But I got such pleasure when my S.G.'s borrowed it, and I was especially gratified when my dear friend Vera adopted the mink as her winter coat when she stayed in New York for three months last winter. The mink story highlights a key element of conjuring. You never know exactly how your conjuring will be made use of, but if you enjoy every drop of your conjurings, from conception to delivery, they always benefit everyone they touch. Conjurings never cost money. They are living tributes to your power to attract.

Sometimes conjurings don't happen right away, but never fear, there are little markers along the Sister Goddess highway that tell you you are on the right track. There are buds that don't blossom into flowers, but they lead to the flower. For example, the very day that S.G. Greta, who works in merchandizing for a large chain of clothing stores, decided that she wanted a new job, she went out for a drink with her girlfriend and ran into someone who works for Banana Republic. This fellow gave S.G. Greta his card and said he was looking for someone in merchandizing. Now Greta wasn't interested in working there, but she knew this was a sign of something to come. It meant that she was right to be looking for a job change and that she was moving in a good direction. S.G. Greta eventually got a job at a place that was far better suited to her desires than Banana Republic would have been.

Another goddess, S.G. Lorna, was looking for a boyfriend. She met this guy Gary who she thought was "the one." She had a few great dates with him, and then he started to cancel dates with her and retreat. At first Lorna was hurt and upset, but then she decided that Gary's exit meant he was simply a harbinger of "the one." Indeed he was. The next guy who came into this S.G's life was a blind date named Stan, who flew in for the weekend on his private plane just to meet her. Stan and Lorna had an incredible time together. Since they met several months ago, these two have flown to the Bahamas together and have embarked upon an unbelievable love affair. Lorna is grateful to Gary for showing her she was on the right track, and she is even more grateful for Stan. S.G. Lorna realizes that Gary helped to get her juices flowing.

You call on the power of desire to create anything you want, independent of the price tag or the apparent impossibility of attainment.

Undeterred by the odds, challenges, or cost, your desires conjure away. The only condition is that your desire be authentic. It doesn't work when you are trying to measure up to someone else's standards or impress someone or prove yourself. Your conjuring power kicks in only for your real, true, deep desires.

One of my goddesses, S.G. Blair, a dermatologist, was stymied during the discussion of desire's power of attraction. She told me she wanted to marry a rich guy and be on the boards of a lot of charities. But much as she focused on this wish, Blair was getting nowhere, and she was getting angrier and angrier. S.G. Blair was angry that she wasn't meeting the right guys, angry that women who were younger than she was were meeting the right guys. Let me just say that Ms. Blair was generally pissed at everyone and everything. Well, when she explained to Mama why she wanted what she wanted, the problem became clear. Blair said she felt marrying Mr. Megabucks was the appropriate next step for a woman of her age—forty-three—and level of accomplishments. She didn't necessarily want a man; she wanted to prove to the world that she made the right choices. The truth was that Blair could barely keep on friendly terms with even her dry cleaner, she was so angry at men. So it was no surprise that no conjuring was happening for her. She thought establishing herself socially was a real, inner desire. She thought that marrying up was what she wanted. But in fact, Blair had still not tapped into her true yearnings.

Most of us have a habit of considering what we possess to be insufficient. That creates a kink in the hose, a crimp in our ability to have more. The reason Blair found no guy was that she disapproved of the fact that she was still single at forty-three. Blair thought she should have had a guy already, and she thought every guy she met should be way better, way richer, way more established than he was already. She would have to get happy with being single first. She would have to attend to her happiness and make that a first priority.

When you start practicing you will begin to see evidence of your conjurings everywhere. Remember S.G. Jillian from Lesson 2? She was the one who turned down that art show in Paris and in so doing made the space to conjure one here in New York. And S.G. Avis—she wanted a baby. Avis was ogling at and enjoying everyone's babies for about a year. At a party she met Trent, who was a renowned obstetrician. Within a month of dating him, Avis was pregnant. What happened was that S.G. Avis experienced a very fast conjuring, after a year of salivating.

The desire you have is of primary importance. Just do whatever you can think of to make way for your desire to do its thing. Once, when I wanted to go to Jamaica on vacation, I told Bruce about it. We had absolutely no money. But we called a travel agent, got brochures, looked at Web sites, inquired about flights, and generally soaked ourselves in information. What we were doing with our information gathering was taking relevant steps. What happened to us was that a wealthy client was so pleased with the results of our work, he gave us a $10,000 tip. It was more than we needed to go on that island vacation.

It's important, once you take on the mantle of a Sister Goddess, to be disciplined about acknowledging the bounty you encounter. This acknowledgment muscle is pretty weak in most of my S.G.'s, to start. We are not accustomed to being in a state of profound gratitude toward our lives and the gift of life. But gratitude is an essential practice that opens us up for more—more love, more stuff, more of whatever we want.

I usually notice that, by approximately week four in my Womanly Arts class, the originally hungry Goddesses are now starting to feel a little stuffed with goodies. That, of course, is my goal. But what I teach along with the methods for getting these goodies is the way to keep them coming. And that way is acknowledgment. For good is not good enough for a Sister Goddess. Continually creating and fulfilling the vision of something better is way more fun, and you can create that by upping your acknowledgments.

If you are not constantly saying, "Thank you, Goddess!" or thank you to whoever contributed to you, you will stop the flow of good from coming your way. S.G. Vivienne, who just visited my "Training Your Man" class, shared with the group that she was constantly acknowledging and appreciating her husband, even when he just picked up the baby or fed the cat. This gal is on the right track. Even though the cat and the baby are her and her husband's shared responsibilities, thanking her guy gave Vivienne pleasure and ensured future rewards. Like her, you should keep the gifts in your life front and center with an expression of thanks for them.

If a Sister Goddess acknowledges what she has and appreciates it, she will get more. S.G. Lucy, a gal who has been with me since my classes began, learned this lesson the hard way. For a long time she did not even acknowledge herself. She was forty-five years old and had never been married. Suddenly there was this young, handsome, sexy guy who adored her and wanted to make her happy and marry her. S.G. Lucy did not do her goddessly homework, she did not acknowledge what a really big deal this was for her. So, instead of being able to move forward into the next level of fun, she slid backward.

S.G. Lucy was on a real roll before her backsliding caught up with her. She used the lessons she learned in her Goddess classes to put together a great business, create a nice savings plan and investments, repair her relationship with her family, and start dating Todd. S.G.

Lucy was doing great. She had a lot to be thankful for. After she had been dating this Todd for a year or so, he wanted to move in with her. But it was at this point that S.G. Lucy couldn't handle all the positive things that had flooded into her life. The love and attention her boyfriend gave her and acted upon with his proposal of moving in together was the final straw. She flipped! It was too much intimacy, too much commitment. Suddenly, in Lucy's eyes, her boyfriend's flaws began to expand—he didn't make enough money, he smoked, he had a potbelly.

S.G. Lucy was caught in a downward spiral. She stopped coming to class. She dwelled on what was wrong with this guy, rather than on what was right. There was a lot right. Todd worshiped the ground Lucy walked on. He was completely committed to pleasuring her and making her happy. Todd was also willing to move from Washington to New York to be with her, change his career, stop smoking, lose weight—basically this guy was willing to do whatever would make S.G. Lucy happy. Frankly, this is what overwhelmed our gal Lucy.

Now, Mama has a saying, "Unacknowledged good turns to shit!" This was an amazing example of that. S.G. Lucy had never had a guy love her as much as Todd did. She was not used to the kind of attention he was giving her, and her way of coping was to refuse to see it. Lucy failed to appreciate him properly.

Acknowledgment works in a similar way to chewing and swallowing. If you are eating dinner, you have to chew and swallow your mouthful before you can have another. When you acknowledge, you consume, or chew and swallow, the wonderful bite you just received, and you are ready for the next one. No chewing and swallowing, and there will be no next bite—your mouth is only so big. When Lucy failed to acknowledge the goodness in her guy and in herself, she was unable to consume any more of what he had to offer her. Their relationship became worse and worse until they finally broke up. Lucy will have to get more skilled in the goddessly art of acknowledging if she ever wants more in the relationship department.

Now, because I know the necessity of thanks, I am an acknowledgment machine. I deeply appreciate and give thanks for everything—the food on my table, the opportunities of living here in the United States of America, my health, my family, my friends, and my life. When you start noticing your own abundance, it grows. The gift of life is overwhelmingly wonderful. We all have so much to be thankful for. Acknowledgment is a fantastic and necessary tool in a S.G.'s toolbox. Don't forget to use it regularly.

You know that expression, "It's not easy being queen"? Well, with the maintenance plan and all of this acknowledgment pressure, are you getting the feeling that it's not easy being queen? If so, I'd have to agree with you. It takes way more responsibility to enjoy your life than to complain about it. It takes way more responsibility to handle your pleasure than to be angry at other people because you are not getting yours. It takes way more responsibility to investigate your desires than to blame others because your dreams haven't come true.

There is no such thing as failure when you pursue your inner desires. The only failure, as far as Mama is concerned, is compromise and mediocrity. We are taught to do things for money, rather than love. Becoming a lawyer, or an accountant, or a secretary just to make your rent does not make the world a better place or you a happier person. Living your dream does. There is limitless possibility in this world—go out and get your vision of success and happiness! If you do what you want, you will get what you want. Here are some exercises that will help you see and make your way toward those true desires that live large in your heart.

Exercise 1: Wallow in Your Desires

Enjoy the desires you have. Don't edit them or say, "I love that dress, but I can't afford it." Just love what you love, want what you want. Take yourself shopping to places where you can just relish the enjoyment of your desires. Try on a fur at a fur salon! If you begin to enjoy your desires, they expand. Maybe your desires head in a different direction. S.G. Stephanie came to New York because she loves theater. She began by saying *yes* to any theater job she was offered, just for the thrill of being backstage. Six months later, she had her first paying job as a stage manager because she allowed herself to wallow in what she loves.

A true Sister Goddess can expand her world by focusing on what she wants and appreciating what she has. The goal we work toward as Sister Goddesses is our ability to give the universe the opportunity to answer our desires, rather than to limit ourselves with our own financial status. When you treat yourself like the queen you want to become, you cultivate a state of contentment in what you have, while being able to envision the possibility of attaining your goals. This is the way of the Sister Goddess.

Exercise 2: The Book of Desires

Get an empty scrapbook and fill it with pictures from magazines of all the fabulous things or experiences you desire, without worrying about the price tag. When you're done, you'll have an entire catalogue of your desires. It's really fun to share this book with friends! Be brave! If you need help, look at the laws of desire outlined in *The Game of Life and How to Play It,* by Florence Scovel Shinn, written in the 1920s by a woman who knew the power of desire! Read this wonderful book!

Exercise 3: Improve Your Karma — Give to Get

Do anonymous acts of good. Do some charity work. Once you give to others, you grow more in touch with how much you have. Goodness begets goodness. Identify and pursue your dreams fervently, and get ready to be surprised by the wealth of fulfilled wishes that come your way.

Exercise 4: Video Suggestion

A Little Princess, directed by Alfonso Cuarón. Watch and be inspired at how this young girl uses her desires to conjure wonderful things for her friends and family. She has no doubts! She holds tightly to her dreams in the face of many obstacles. Let her inspire you.

* * *

Well, yo' mama has given her all. You, my divine novitiates, are in possession, now, of the keys to the Queendom. The road map to ecstasy has been charted. The question is: Will you take the plunge?

Lesson 10

The Sister Goddess Study Guide

Pussy, Pussy, she's my queen,
She will lead me to my dream.
—Ancient Sister Goddess Womantra

There are going to be a handful of you who will read every word of this magnificent discourse and will still wonder, "Huh?" or think, "Why bother?" or, "I'm too far gone, anyway," or, "That's all well and good, but I have to go back to work now." Mama has a special soft spot for all of you. Being a hard nut herself, she knows: the harder the nut, the sweeter the meat. So, sweeties, this chapter is for all of you.

We all are just so set in our ways. We have the most profound attachment to our little predictable methods of doing things. I am so mad for my way of making my coffee in the morning that I actually have to take a cup of it with me in a thermos when I go to my favorite brunch spot. They tolerate me. They know I hate their coffee. My crazy method keeps me from coffee I hate, but do you think it could ever keep me from coffee that's actually better than what I brew at home? You betcha. I started hauling my thermos everywhere, like a blankie. I knew I had gone over the edge when I ended up taking my home brew to a café. Yes, I toted my thermos right into a place that actually specializes in expresso, cappuccino, you know, the whole world of coffee. And there I was, with my blankie. At this point, I hid blankie in my knapsack and I ordered a café au lait. It came in beautiful large stemware, with a thick layer of foam on top. Ah . . . And that's all I'm asking you, gals. Ditch your blankies, reach for the stemware.

Your blankies are your old, logical conditioning. You find yourself shaking your head and wrinkling your nose in disdain and saying, in an English accent, inside your own head, "Oh no . . . I would never do *that!* That simply is not acceptable!" Your "never" may be pleasuring yourself, it may be looking at your Pussy, it may be writing a love letter to yourself, it may be dancing naked, it may be asking for something you want from a man. Lord only knows . . . But Mama will tell you—the things in this book that you find yourself resisting the most are where the biggest goodies are, *for you.*

If I had to post a warning sign on the Womanly Arts highway, it would be this: *NO COASTING.* There is only one direction you roll when you coast, and that is downhill. What I mean by coasting is thinking that because you read this book, or because you took the class, you are automatically, and forever, a Sister Goddess. The truth is you are a Sister Goddess only as long as you continue practicing the Womanly Arts that got you to the land of the Goddess in the first place—like pleasuring yourself, continually and exuberantly; telling the truth to people, especially men, and not expecting them to read your mind; acknowledging the good that comes your way; and continuing to view where you are as a fantastic place, even as you envision higher ground.

To help you stick to the Womanly Arts, let's take a look at what happened to one Sister Goddess who became lax in her pursuit of personal pleasure. Let me tell you, it ain't pretty. While she started out as a model Goddess, S.G. Elizabeth forgot about her Womanly Arts maintenance plan, and soon found herself in dating paralysis. When she first came to class, Elizabeth began pampering herself, indulging herself, and generally having fun. Whoops! A flood of guys appeared, asking her out, buying her drinks, whatever. She was overwhelmed. But she kept up with those Womanly Arts!

After dating a slew of eligible guys, Elizabeth settled on a cute one named Philip. For a while, she maintained her goddessly standards and everything unfolded nicely. S. G. Elizabeth dated other guys, too. She kept going out with her girlfriends and treating herself well.

But about four months into the relationship, Elizabeth replaced her relationship with the Goddess with her relationship with the guy. He became her god. She did what he wanted, went where he wanted to go, ate what he liked to eat. S. G. Elizabeth was so swept up with making the relationship with Philip work that she forgot to keep her own pleasure in mind.

What happened? Elizabeth became disinterested in the relationship and started hating Philip, the guy she so clearly felt deeply about. Why did this happen? S.G. Elizabeth forgot to keep her own internal flame burning. Yes, Elizabeth allowed herself to go on autopilot instead of making a conscious decision to practice her Womanly Arts. Oops!

Of course, Elizabeth broke up with Philip and went through a really miserable period—until she started remembering that there was a time, not so far back, that she was feeling really good. Then our gal Elizabeth got back in touch with what got her to that feel-good place—her Womanly Arts lessons. S.G. Elizabeth vows to never forget them again.

Like Elizabeth, you may have noticed that life without the Womanly Arts of fun and beauty and flirtation is no picnic. Life without your pleasure as a priority is one of perpetual victimization and stagnation. As you also may also have realized, a life of pleasure is not exactly a free ride. Your practice of the Womanly Arts requires a rigorous, internal discipline that rewards you exponentially for the investment you make in yourself and your desires. You can't expect to have a fabulous body without working out. Likewise, you can't expect to cut loose the magic, thrill-a-minute, goddessly side of you without similar care and vigilance when it comes to your own self-pleasuring.

You can become as addicted to pleasure as you once were to mediocrity, compromise, and doubt. But the habit of going to the gym, say, is way more difficult to sustain than the habit of reaching for the bag of Cheetos and the bag of Oreos. Your conditioning is so powerful that it might very well convince you to return to your self-cheatin' ways with one inner thought, like, "Yea honey, go eat that bag of chips, forget about the orgasm."

So, there are definitely times when you'll have to be strong. Being a Sister Goddess means saying, "I am worth more to myself and the world when I am pleasured," and taking the time to indulge yourself—no matter what the obstacles. There is great reward if you dedicate yourself to pleasure. Think about it. If you look back over your life from right now, your most memorable moment won't be your overeating or working too hard or denying yourself. If you're like me, your most memorable moments will be the kisses you gave in to and other vivid and lush sensual experiences, exquisite dinners with friends, travel excursions to exotic places, the passionate flirtations you had, the scent of your lover's body, and the overwhelming beauty of the ocean at dawn. All the risks and rewards of pleasure.

Take it from me, the risks are worth it. Do you think that when I started my journey, I *wanted* to end up running Pussy Central, U.S.A.? Do you think I *wanted* my job to be all about the sensual unfolding of women? Don't you think I wished it could all be about something way, way more socially acceptable? Believe me, I tried *everything* else. But this Womanly Arts thing changed my life.

Sometimes it is extremely difficult, if not impossible, to reach for what you want. You are clinging so tightly to your blankies that you completely miss the waiter coming around with the tray of cafés au lait or lattes. That is where your Sister Goddess network proves to be invaluable. Maintain your own group of women who want only the very best for one another, who want to continue to expand the fun in their lives . . . and in the lives of their S.G.'s. That, my darlings, is the real "New Girl Order."

❋ ❋ ❋

Before we part, I want to remind you of some of the key points we've covered in seeking our Womanly Arts training. Knowing you can turn to the bullion cube of wisdom concentrated here at the end of the book might help you when you are feeling temporarily adrift.

I hope you'll keep this guide handy always and then, when you think your instinct for pleasure might be extinguished by the corrosive influence of the patriarchy that surrounds you, quickly flip to this section and resuscitate your Goddess and her innate wisdom. But of course, you don't have to be on the verge of a masochistic meltdown to benefit from these Womanly Arts highlights. Feel free to browse anytime just to keep your happiness alive, strong, and glowing.

The Womanly Arts Cheat Sheet

- Give yourself pleasure at least once a week. It can be anything that gives you pleasure: a massage, a manicure, a bath or shower with candles, an uninterrupted hour with your feet up and a stack of magazines.
- Honor your body with rituals.
- Brag about yourself at least once a day.
- Don't compromise. Make it your intention to have what you want.
- Invest in yourself. Read a great book, exercise, take a walk by yourself.
- Experience sensual pleasure. Remember, "You must know pleasure to give pleasure."
- Keep a detailed want list. Add to it continuously. See how it changes as you use your Womanly Arts.
- Maintain your Sister Goddess network.
- Keep acknowledging and giving thanks for all you have.

One last thing, a word from our sponsor. I think if she had a message, and it could be verbalized, our Pussy would say something like this:

I could truly blow your mind,
If you follow my design
And show me a really, really good time.

That's really not a bad deal, gals. In fact, it's the best offer you are ever gonna get. And just what, exactly, have you got to lose?

Love,
Mama